BARB OF FIRE

NIHIL OBSTAT:
Monsignor Philip Loftus, BCL

IMPRIMATUR:
Monsignor Michael R. Quinlan, DCL, V.G.
Salford, 19 July 2001

BARB OF FIRE

Twenty Poems of Blessed Elizabeth of the Trinity

Translated by Alan Bancroft,
with selected passages from
BLESSED COLUMBA MARMION

First published in 2001

Gracewing
2 Southern Ave, Leominster
Herefordshire HR6 0QF

ISBN 0 85244 542 3

Typesetting by Action Publishing Technology Ltd.,
Gloucester, GL1 5SR

Printed by MPG Books Ltd.,
Bodmin PL31 1EG

CONTENTS

Acknowledgements

I wish to express warm gratitude for the immense practical help and encouragement given to me by Sœur Marie-Michelle de la Croix, OCD, Prioress of the Dijon Carmel at Flavignerot, and by Dom Mark Tierney, OSB, of Glenstal Abbey, Co. Limerick, Vice-Postulator of the Beatification Cause of the, now, Blessed Columba Marmion.

I wish also to acknowledge the kindness of Dom Ferdinand Poswick, OSB, of Maredsous Abbey, Vice-Postulator, and to thank Dom Gregory Collins, OSB, of Glenstal Abbey, who in the midst of other time-consuming activities read this book in its early form and who helped me greatly on important points.   A.B.

To Mary

Then, Barb of Fire, pierce also now through us!
(Elizabeth)

*The Trinity is God: God is the Trinity; the Trinity . . . is
our everlasting joy and bliss.*
(Mother Julian of Norwich)

TRANSLATOR'S INTRODUCTION

These words are about an individual and about the cosmic. About the purposed and eternal place of that individual, Elizabeth, and the place offered similarly to every other individual, in an actuality both unending and tremendous. Saints – that is, persons we formally honour as such or as 'Blessed' and those unhonoured by name because the extent of their response is not universally known to us – did not merely refrain from rejecting their destiny and inheritance. (It *can* be rejected, love including God's can be rejected,[1]* though it is an immense folly for someone knowingly to risk the permanent losing of that eternal inheritance for some continuing or other advantage that is short-term, like all our life in the present world.) Far from merely not rejecting, which is a negative thing, the saints *rushed* – or maybe they plodded determinedly – to arms wide-out to receive them.

One refers to human destiny, eternal inheritance. When he was still Archbishop of Cracow, two years before he became John Paul II, Cardinal Karol Wojtyla gave a series of addresses in a Lenten Retreat attended by Pope Paul VI and others at Rome. In two of his addresses the future Pope gave much emphasis to a passage from Vatican II (*Gaudium et Spes*, n.22): 'Christ, who is the new Adam, by revealing the mystery of the Father and his love, also *fully reveals man to man himself and makes his exalted vocation known to him*'.[2]

*The numbers in this Introduction refer to the Notes beginning on p. 188.

1

Blessed Elizabeth

Marie Elizabeth Catez, who had a firm and strong desire to enter the Carmelite convent at Dijon, was once asked by a friend of her mother's what she could find to say during the long periods when she was praying to God in Church. 'Oh, madame,' she replied, 'we love one another!'[3]

Such ingenuous simplicity reminds one of St Thérèse of Lisieux; and since the very circumstances of their lives invite a comparison, let us begin by comparing, as persons – albeit with an extreme of sketchiness – St Thérèse and Blessed Elizabeth of the Trinity, as we now call the girl who gave that reply. The external events of the two lives were remarkably similar, but when we go on to consider Elizabeth's thought as set out in her writings we are in country which, for all the similarities we find there, is distinctively her own. (Her own, in the sense that she illuminated it with her own personality; and yet in giving her perceptions what she always seeks to expound is, not any novel ideas of her own, but firm biblical teaching and Catholic tradition. 'You can believe my doctrine', she said in writing about the Divine indwelling 'for it is not mine',[4] not my own idea.)

Both young women lived in France towards the end of the nineteenth century. Both came from comfortable bourgeois families. Each lost one of her parents when young.[5] Both entered Carmelite convents and died at an early age after illness; Thérèse at twenty-four, Elizabeth (from Addison's disease, then incurable) at twenty-six. Both left writings which have enriched us.

One commentator[6] has remarked on an apparent difference shown by their photographs. Thérèse, he says, 'looks merry, Elizabeth happy'. I would add that the latter's writings, though certainly coming from the prayer and inspiration of the moment, give to me the appearance of less spontaneity than Thérèse's. Elizabeth does not sparkle in the delightful way

Thérèse so frequently does, but her writings could perhaps be described as more cerebral.[7] Those dark eyes, large pensive and still, gaze out at you from her photographs and you feel you are looking into very deep pools. Her writings are no less deep and inspired for being expressed in words formed through a weighing-up of her intellect.

And yet we are not talking about a very learned person, albeit that she was highly intelligent, articulate and perceptive. When she adopted a motto-name for herself – a name to which we shall return, 'Praise of Glory' – she took from St Paul, in the Latin, the phrase 'Laudem Gloriae', without realising (it seems) that grammatically 'Laudem' is the accusative case – 'in laudem gloriae', 'unto the praise of glory'. The correct nominative would have been 'Laus' Gloriae. But, as a Jesuit Father wrote about this: 'Happy are the souls who have only faults of grammar to regret!'[8]

Nor was Elizabeth trained in theology.[9] But it is not learning that brings about or indicates wisdom and sanctity.

Or sanity. In his book *Theology and Sanity*, Frank Sheed explained what he meant by the last word of its title. Most of us, we have to admit, are only partially sane. Sanity, Sheed wrote, 'does not mean living in the same world as everyone else; it means living in the real world.'[10]

If, in spite of our notional, intellectual, acceptance that eternity awaits us after death – if our actions and our assumptions are in practice geared to the position that our death is simply a termination of everything, or that our after-life is an appendage of merely secondary importance to our life here, then we are out of touch not just with Christian piety but *with reality*. The actual fact, which we may not recognize or which in our fey human way we may put aside, is not merely that death is the gateway to eternity, but that the nature of our individual eternity matters IN FACT more than anything else, for (astonishing this concept is when we ponder it!) eternity, being endless, is literally for ever. Unlike God, we each had a beginning. Like God, however, we shall not have an end, for that is how God created the 'me' that is the individual person.

If our loves are both set on and limited to the evanescent if not the tawdry, what is to be said of our grasp upon reality?

Except when we are old, the life we are now living seems long, because we see it from our viewpoint within it. But bring in the perspective of eternity as a backdrop to our thought, and this affects remarkably and radically not only our attitude to our individual destiny but also our approach to questions such as those beginning 'Why does God allow . . .?' For something that would undoubtedly be a complete disaster if the present life were everything may not be the *same* in the scale of disaster or its absence considered relative to eternal outcome. (In the circumstances of some disasters, the factor of causation by human free will – free will that God leaves inviolate in us – enters in; but that is a separate point.) By looking at such questions against the vista of infinity we can – not exactly solve them (for during this life the answers are hidden in mystery), but at least widen out what is understandably our telescoped, our 'tunnel', vision. With that wider vision we can see a possibility, at least, that the ship will come safe to a harbour where all will be splendidly well. Lazarus can become Dives – Dives the rich – in eternity.

Though the perspective of eternity – its vast difference from seventy, eighty, a hundred years – does objectively alter both the general and speculative questions as well as the personal ones, the real difficulty for us, obviously, lies in our being able actually to abstract ourselves in thought from this week and next week, next year and the year after. Those times are the times of our being tested; but they are also what, according to our human nature, impact upon us now. Today and next year are what we feel and touch.

In Sheed's sense Elizabeth, like all the saints, was wholly sane. With a knowledge and an understanding infused into the 'bones' of her soul, she knew what ultimately matters. In the same way, the framer of the old Litany of Jesus had a sane perspective when he wrote: 'Teach us to endure all things for everlasting happiness'.

Unreservedness

How does it come about, a saint's *rushing* to grasp the Love of God? In the love between God and individuals it is not we who make the first move. Without the grace of God, who 'loved us first',[11] we can do nothing. This applies to the smallest, the most tenuous, manifestation of love from ourselves. But what of, not the trickle but the flood? If we are to credit the great saints who were the founders of Elizabeth's Reformed Order, it is generosity, unreservedness, in the sense of a willingness to hold nothing back – something which God sees and foreknows will be the active response to His grace – that calls forth such torrents of grace as cause a saint to say, and obviously to think, 'Oh, I do nothing and God does everything'. St Teresa of Avila wrote: 'The chief point is that we should resolutely give Him our heart for His own ... As Christ does not force our will, He only takes what we give Him, but He does not give Himself entirely until He sees that we yield ourselves entirely to Him ... Nor does He work within the soul to the same extent when it is not wholly given to Him ...'[12] St John of the Cross said that God establishes His grace and love in a soul 'in proportion to the good will of that soul's love'.[13]

In Elizabeth, as in Thérèse, we see unreservedness personified.

During infancy she had been subject to strong bursts of temper, which her mother's loving but firm psychology caused her to control. Her First Confession and Communion at nearly eleven marked what others said was a visible change in her: she became completely gentle (*d'une douceur exemplaire*), though sometimes there were signs of an inward struggle against her former temper, described as violent. She was a child pianist, and it seems in keeping with her fiery nature that she had, people said, a 'brilliant and expressive' style.

But even before her First Communion – four years before that – she had, it seems, formed an intention for the future. Heaven knows what human circumstance (or maybe it was wholly an infusion by God, who knows future dispositions and receptivity) had put the idea into her little head. An old Canon of Carcassone, a friend of the family, records that she clambered on to his knee and whispered, 'Canon, I am going to be a nun! I want to be a nun.' 'I believe she was seven years old!', he wrote. 'What is the silly little thing saying?', her mother asked the Canon.

We have a prayer, addressed to her patroness, St Elizabeth of Hungary, which she composed at thirteen. It asks for 'your beautiful virtues, your sweet humility and your sublime charity. Obtain from God His changing of my faults into virtues . . .'

These details are taken from the *Souvenirs*,[14] reminiscences of her published in 1909, three years after her death. A priest who became her spiritual director described her piety as 'really natural in its supernaturality; no intense excitement, nothing of the extra-ordinary driving her'. But the *Souvenirs* say this remarkable thing, based on her early diaries: 'Already the dear child showed herself avid for immolation . . .' This is perhaps an unusual craving, at an early or any other age. It needs further comment, and we shall return to it.

She wrote that from childhood she had determined 'to be wholly God's'.[15] That 'wholly', about the gift of herself, was

6

not a rhetorical phrase; she meant it. Receptivity and grace, grace and receptivity, were combining towards a life-long attitude, a life-long active love that is indeed to be wondered at (and yet is not incapable of being imitated, through grace, at any stage of our own lives). The *Souvenirs* say: 'She could not understand how people could give themselves by halves to the good God.' Her call to an unreserved giving was through the vocation of being a Carmelite nun. Our life-vocation may be wholly different, but then the call to a giving without reservation is in those different circumstances of ours. Mostly not easy, yet we have to try; and every effort in that direction upon earth (as distinguished from the later cleansing and waiting of Purgatory) must surely be accounted as worth the making, for the End and the Prize is great.

'Disappearance' of self

But, true as all that is, we omit something vital from Elizabeth's message if we present the picture simply as a calculated effort, even a calculated loving effort, to attain the fulfilment of self in eternity. What she urges is the destruction of self, in the sense that, by conforming our desires and our will completely to God's desires and will we are (if one may put it so) left with God's desires and will *only*, these being deliberately adopted by us as our desires and will out of love for Him: 'not my will but Yours be done'.[16] In heaven, loving unreservedly will not be difficult, we cannot do otherwise: if one may so express it, the soul's heart will surge up at the first sight of the Reality – the Beauty, Magnificence and Love – that is God. But here below, in the darkness of faith – well, not so easy, since one's own self wants to make itself the centre and reality. Yet Elizabeth's message is that that sinking, that 'forgetting', of self is possible here below, and we had better make a start on it:

7

> ... A drop of water, lost
>   in such a mighty sea!
> Grant, all that's not divine
>   destroy in me, that so
> Into your Being, swift
>   my soul can then rush free.[17]

That is not to say that we can ever lose the individual personality with which God the Creator endowed us; it is simply to say how that individual personality achieves the fulfilment for which it was created.

That image, the drop of water and the great sea, appears in St Thérèse's account of her First Communion (which account Elizabeth had read). Thérèse wrote that Jesus and 'poor little Thérèse' looked at and understood each other. 'That day, it was no longer a look, but a *fusion*, there were no longer two, Thérèse had disappeared, like a drop of water lost in the heart of the ocean.' In *The Living Flame of Love*, St John of the Cross had written: 'This is why the Psalmist said, "Precious in the sight of the Lord is the death of His saints",[18] *for then the rivers of the soul flow into the sea of love* ...'[19]

We should note, however, that abandon − Thérèse and Elizabeth entrusting themselves wholly to God − *doesn't* mean giving up effort oneself. Loving is more than allowing oneself to be loved. The spiritual lives of both these holy persons showed that an active response was involved in 'I love You, I give myself to You for ever.'[20]

It is in such a deep context, then − breathtaking when one thinks of it − that Elizabeth says the pretensions of one's internal imposter have to be suppressed. 'A soul which holds dialogue with its self, which occupies itself with its feelings, which pursues useless thoughts, desires of some sort − that soul scatters its forces, it is not wholly disposed in order toward God. Its lyre does not vibrate in unison, and when the Master touches this lyre He cannot bring forth celestial harmonies, it has still too much of the human, it is a dissonance.' The soul 'must continually retune the strings of its instrument which everywhere are a little out'.[21]

What, in fact, does Elizabeth say Elizabeth-in-journey should do? Well, actually, that Elizabeth should *disappear*. She insists on the need to 'forget' one's self – and she uses numerous other words and phrases for the same idea: to be 'separated from', 'go out from', 'despise', 'leave', 'withdraw from', 'lose sight of', 'die to', be 'emancipated from', 'break with', 'master', 'renounce', 'sacrifice', 'destroy', 'abase', be 'unconscious of', 'oblivious of', 'free from', 'stripped of', 'above', 'wholly delivered from', 'detached from' self. These are translators' renderings of terms used by Elizabeth.[22] How extraordinary! Could there be something in what she says?

It is extremely important, I think, that we do not mistake her meaning. In wanting the 'self' to disappear and be immersed in God, she is not seeking some pantheistic loss of identity. When St Paul said 'now not I', he prefaced that phrase with an assertion of his continuing identity as Paul: '*I* live, now not I, but Christ liveth in me.'[23] When in ordinary speech we say that so-and-so is 'a different person', it is still of so-and-so that we speak.

Then, what *is* that 'self' which must disappear? Related to how one's free will is exercised, the 'self' (which is to be annihilated) is an amalgam of everything that is displeasing to God and therefore may be said to be Elizabeth-apart-from-God rather than Elizabeth at one with, united with, God. The latter Elizabeth, but not the former, dwells in 'a truly spacious place'.[24]

The disappearance of which she speaks involves the free subordination of her own will, through love. '. . . the more (a person) annihilates self for God, in sense and spirit', wrote St John of the Cross,[25] 'the more will he be united with God, and the greater the work he will accomplish.' 'It seems to me', Elizabeth remarked, 'that saints are souls who forget themselves all the time, who lose themselves . . . in Him whom they love, without returning upon self . . .'[26]

The Divine Indwelling

A reiterated part of Elizabeth's message is that on the subject of the 'dwelling' of the Blessed Trinity in the soul of a person in grace. Of course, it is simply a restatement, a salutary re-emphasis, of Christ's own words: 'If any one love me, he will keep my word, and my Father will love him, and we will come to him, and will make our abode with him' (John 14:23) and other remarkable biblical texts.

What Blessed Elizabeth did, through the grace of God, was to take those words and that actuality and hold them up for us like a jewel. When the above text, so deep and so important, is mentioned in the *Catechism of the Catholic Church* and an illustration is desired of a state of mind to which the Divine presence in the soul gave rise in loving alertness to 'Your creative action' and will, it is Elizabeth's words that have been chosen. The Catechism (260) says that the ultimate end of the whole divine economy is 'the entry of God's creatures into the perfect unity of the Blessed Trinity. But even now (it continues) we are called to be a dwelling for the Most Holy Trinity.' And then follows the great text of John 14:23, and underneath it the first five sentences of Elizabeth's Prayer to the Trinity, 'O my God, Trinity whom I adore . . .'

In letter after letter she wrote about the Divine indwelling: 'the God who dwells in her . . . is more present to her than she is to herself'; 'He is within us to sanctify us'; 'He who is to judge us lives within us to save us all the time from our miseries . . .'; 'He dwells in the innermost centre

10

of your soul as if in a sanctuary where unceasingly He wants to be loved to adoration.'[27]

Note the *mutuality* of indwelling expressed in another saying of Christ's recorded in the Gospels: 'Abide in me: and I in you'.[28] Elizabeth's own language echoes that deeply-significant element of mutuality: '... passed wholly into [Christ], and He into me', she wrote in her *Last Retreat*.[29] Elsewhere she spoke of 'the soul (which) flows into God, while God flows into it so as to transform it into Himself'.[30]

To see why the Divine indwelling is not an esoteric idea for mystics only, we have to consider, first, something which most certainly is not thus restricted, namely the Catholic doctrine of 'supernatural life'. 'Supernatural' tends to suggest to us the haunting of houses, but 'super' is simply the Latin for 'above'; and 'supernatural life', also called sanctify-ing grace, is a life (the possibility and offer of which have been made known to us by Christ) that is utterly above our natural life. It 'is *a participation in the life of God*. It introduces us into the intimacy of Trinitarian life' (CCC, para. 1997). It comes to us by baptism, in which term is included, for the salvation of many people in the world, the implicit 'baptism of desire'.[31] It can be lost by grave sin knowingly committed, deliberately consented to; and can be regained, as long as our earthly life lasts, through repentance. If we possess it in our souls at death we have achieved our destiny, for we shall certainly then see God face to face in heaven, achieving thereby utter happiness for ever (though for those who indeed possess supernatural life in their souls at death but still fall short of the spiritual perfection needed for union with God in heaven there will be a period of waiting in the cleans-ing-place or condition called purgatory).

Such in essence is Catholic doctrine. Though believing it whole-heartedly, one can take a superficial view of what supernatural life really means. Is supernatural life imper-sonal, like something out of a box or bottle labelled 'the life

11

of Christ'? No, it is not. It is a glorious *personal* extension to oneself – Personal in the giving, and personal to oneself the receiver – of the Love which the Three Persons of the Blessed Trinity have eternally for each other. '. . . we will come to him, and will make our abode with him'. I do not know how to characterize this 'presence' further (do the theologians either, even the greatest of them, this being a subject shrouded in mystery?); I do not really or other than dimly know what it means in detail and in practice, but those words of Christ refer to something *personal* between the Divine Persons and the individual soul, do they not?

It is easy to think of Christ, Second Person of the Trinity made man, as personal. But God the Father-Creator is not a Life Force only, not impersonal (though, since He does not have a body, He does not have a beard as many think). As regards personhood, the point of reference is God, and not ourselves. We were made in the 'image and likeness' of God, not God in ours. Nor is God the Father impersonal in regard to *us*: 'That divine office which Jesus Christ received from His Father for the welfare of mankind, and most perfectly fulfilled', wrote Leo XIII, 'has for its final object to put men in possession of the eternal life of glory, and . . . to secure to them the life of divine grace which is destined eventually to blossom into the life of heaven.'[32]

Personal love

When St John the Evangelist wrote 'God is love'[33] (not merely 'is loving', for this is Absolute Love) he was not referring to something impersonal. We know from revelation of the infinite love of the eternal Father for His eternal Son, of God the eternal Son for His eternal Father. And the Holy Spirit, who eternally 'proceeds from the Father and the Son',[34] *is* in some mysterious way the Love between the

Father and the Son, between the Son and the Father – though He, the Spirit, is a distinct Divine Person. One God, three Persons.[35] Not impersonal, therefore, this eternal love. *Amans, Amatus, Amor*, the Lover, the Loved One, and the Love. God is love in three Divine Persons.

St John of the Cross, with the insight of a poet (and perhaps also through some direct perception, partial and momentary, as the mystic he was) wrote, in a poem on the communion of love of the three Divine Persons, of '*words of an infinite rapture*' within the Trinity:

> What of them we can sense the clearest
> Was in this manner said and thought:
> Out of Your company, my Dearest,
> I can be satisfied by nought.[36]

When Christ, the Second Person of the Blessed Trinity made man, says 'Abide in me, and I in you', He is opening up to *us* the dimension of a participation in that Trinitarian life such as might well take the breath away. To be loved by and to love the Triune God eternally, seeing God's ineffable Beauty 'face to face'[37] – not indeed by oneself but with others also 'adopted'[38] gloriously into the life of the Trinity – is what we were created for; our souls (that is, our essential selves[39]) directly and lovingly created by God. Though the vista of Loving-ness is now covered like a mountain by cloud, one who attains to his or her heavenly destiny will thereupon see clearly: 'then', St Paul wrote, 'I shall know even as I am known.'[40] What one will know and experience will have no precedent in its fulfilment and its joy.[41]

. . . . . .

For all the insights of mystical theology, expect from no-one a scientific paper showing how God's action in the indwelling 'works'. In all this we are in the realm of mystery. A mystery, however, is like a tunnel into which

13

we can see only some distance. It is an area of fact about which we know something, and with certainty, but only something.[42]

Some writers on mystical and other prayer use phrases like 'the presence of God returns', when what they are of course referring to is an individual's having a renewed *perception*, or feeling, of God's presence – God making His presence or action to be perceived, felt, by the individual who normally may have no feeling of that presence or action at all. The same writers stress, rightly, that even when a soul that is in grace experiences nothing but a dead and dull feeling of His 'absence', God is in fact present in that soul, working patiently towards the soul's sanctification, moulding, planting. Elizabeth has another repeated metaphor: that of His 'hollowing out abysses' in the soul, greater spaces and capacities to receive Himself.[43] She insisted that God is close to us, 'within', even when He seems very far away.[44]

God's special presence in a soul that is in grace, then, is objective, not subjective.[44a] Our perception of that presence, our loving advertence to it, wholly admirable though the latter is – neither of these things brings into being the presence there, any more than does our awareness of, or our welcoming as opposed to ignoring, someone who is there in our house of bricks and mortar. (It is, indeed, possible for a total absence of feeling to be combined with what Père de Caussade called 'a lasting peace', an unemotional feeling of 'the deeply hidden strength of God's indwelling depth'.[45])

If one does not misunderstand her, Elizabeth seems on one occasion at least to have received a mystical apprehension of, or impress on the mind about, the presence of the Trinity in souls in sanctifying grace. It might be described as a brief perception, obscure still but direct, of what normally believed, though rightly believed, by faith.

Go back three hundred years from Elizabeth's time and consider, first, this passage from the *Relations* of St Teresa of

Avila: 'One Tuesday after the Ascension, having prayed for a while after Communion in great distress, because I was so distracted that I could fix my mind on nothing, I complained of our poor nature to our Lord. The fire began to kindle in my soul, and I saw, as it seemed to me, the Holy Trinity distinctly present in an intellectual vision, whereby my soul understood, through a certain representation, as a figure of the truth, so far as my dullness could understand, how God is Three and One; and thus it seemed to me that all the Three Persons spoke to me, that They were distinctly present in my soul, saying unto me "that from that day forth I should see that my soul had grown better in three ways, and that each one of the Three Persons had bestowed on me a distinct grace – in charity, in suffering joyfully, in a sense of that charity in my soul, accompanied with fervour". I learnt the meaning of those words of our Lord, that the Three Divine Persons will dwell in the soul that is in a state of grace. . . . The vision of the Three Divine Persons – one God – made so profound an impression on my soul that if it had continued it would have been impossible for me not to be recollected in so divine a company. What I saw and heard besides is beyond my power to describe.'[46]

Compare with those words of St Teresa's the following account in the *Souvenirs*, about Elizabeth. On the Feast of the Ascension, the Mother Prioress, visiting Elizabeth in the infirmary and expressing regret at having been delayed in doing so, noticed that her countenance was all transfigured. 'Oh, Mother!', answered the little sick one, 'don't trouble yourself about me. The good God has granted me such a favour that I have lost all idea of time. These words made themselves heard in the depths of my soul this morning: "If any one love me, my Father will love him, and we will come to him". And at the same instant I saw how true it was. I could not say how the Three Divine Persons revealed Themselves, but nevertheless I saw them, holding their council of love within me, and it seems to me that I still see them like that. Oh! how great God is, and how loved we are!'. 'I feel so much that They are there', she said of 'my Divine Guests'.[47]

The two things, the Divine indwelling in a soul in grace and 'supernatural life', are not two subject-areas, but one. 'The Three Divine Persons', writes Père Philipon, OP, 'are substantially present in the soul of a baptized infant who has become, in St Paul's words, "the temple of the Holy Ghost" (1 Cor. 6:19). Our whole spiritual life, from Baptism to the Beatific Vision, develops [or should develop] as a rapidly increasing progressive ascension toward the Trinity.'[48] Writing to her sister before the baptism of the latter's daughter, Elizabeth spoke of the Holy Trinity descending into her baptized niece's soul.[49]

Christ's 'Abide in me: and I in you' is part of His discourse on the Vine and the branches, His instruction on the only way in which the branches will have life and bear fruit and not wither.[50]

Who *are* they who, possessing sanctifying grace at death, will be certain of attaining their eternal inheritance? This rests with Divine Justice and Mercy; and the Church teaches that God wishes all to be saved, for Christ died for all. Those who achieve salvation will include many whose foreheads have not felt the waters of baptism – that is certain. And if it seems difficult to apply the above sublime concepts to some for whom they are no less than an unknown foreign language, one should remember that God, Divine Justice and Divine Mercy, has Divine insight into the individual soul. Certainly none will be penalised for not doing what genuinely they did not feel called on to do.

Elizabeth herself, writing personally, makes personal for us the subject of the Divine indwelling. What she shows us, is that the 'embrace' (her word) of the Trinity's infinite rapture is held out, extended, to us personally. Hans von Balthasar wrote of her: 'She understood it to be her apostolate to infect as many as possible with an immense longing for the infinite'.[51]

The Divine 'Three'

Elizabeth's emphasis, then, is Trinitarian. To speak – as we do with complete accuracy – of the presence of the Holy Spirit in the soul directs the mind to the indwelling of *one of the Persons* of the Trinity. But it does not imply that the Holy Spirit is present to the exclusion of the Father and the Son. Similarly that great text, '. . . we (my Father and I) will come to him', though it mentions only two of the Divine Persons, does not imply an absence of the Holy Spirit. The Holy Spirit, Third Person of the Trinity, *is* the mutual Love between Father and Son, a Love directed to ourselves also.

In his encyclical letter *Divinum illud munus*,[52] on the subject of the Holy Spirit as the soul of the Church, and His dwelling in the souls of the just, Leo XIII wrote that God by grace resides in the just soul as in a temple, in a most intimate and special (*singulari*) manner. 'Now this wonderful union, which is properly called "indwelling", differing only in degree or state from that with which God beatifies the saints in heaven, although it is most certainly produced by the presence of *the whole Blessed Trinity*[53] – "we will come to him, and will make our abode with him" (John 14:23) – nevertheless is attributed[54] in a peculiar [particular] manner to the Holy Ghost. . . . the same Spirit is called holy, for He, the first and supreme Love, moves souls and leads them to sanctity, which ultimately [in the last analysis] consists in the love of God.' Wherefore the Apostle Paul 'when calling us the temple of God (1 Cor. 6:19)[55] does not expressly mention the Father, or the Son, but the Holy Ghost.'

That great Johannine text, recording Christ's 'we will make our abode with him . . .', is frequently quoted without

17

its implications regarding our eternity in the Trinitarian love being dwelt upon. Elizabeth stressed: 'It is the whole Trinity that rests within us, all that mystery which will be our vision in Heaven.'[56] It is an interesting fact that around the turn of the nineteenth century two Carmelite nuns of eminent holiness dwelt upon the text: Elizabeth of the Trinity (who in fact does not in her writings speak exclusively of indwelling by the Three, rather than by one Person of the Three[57]) and – a little in time before Elizabeth, if with less Trinitarian emphasis generally in her works than she – St Thérèse of Lisieux, whose most famous poem, *Living by Love*, begins with a reference to that text:

> In Love's last ev'ning-hours you would have heard
> Jesus say plainly: 'He who would love Me,
> Let him be true, let him obey my Word:
> Father and Son his Visitants shall be.
> Coming, to make his heart a dwelling-place,
> We'll love him always! and Our Peace above
> Shall fill him. For our will it is he stays
>   In our own Love.'

'In her private notes',[58] writes Père Philipon, Elizabeth 'recurs to passages from St John of the Cross which had particularly struck her, especially those from the *Spiritual Canticle*, in which the holy Doctor treats of the nature and effects of the mysterious Divine Presence. There we find the classic doctrine of Catholic theology in a lofty, contemplative light: God is substantially present in all beings by His contact with them as their Creator; to this presence, which is common to all, is added a special presence in the souls of the just [on earth] and in the blessed' in heaven.[59]

This brings out an important point. The term 'presence' of God in created beings can refer simply to God's presence in every person and every thing, or (something immeasurably more intimate) God's presence in the soul of a person who is in grace. On the one hand there is the basic 'presence' of God in every person – as in every inanimate thing like a stone – upholding that person or that thing in existence. St John of the Cross wrote: '. . . we must remember that in every soul, even that of the greatest sinner in the world, God dwells, and is substantially present.' If He were to withdraw this preservation of their being (which in the case of human beings will not happen!), they would at once cease to have any existence at all. 'This way of union or presence of God, in the order of nature, subsists between Him and all his creatures.'

'And so', continues St John of the Cross, 'when I speak of the union of the soul with God, I do not mean this substantial presence which is in every creature, but that union and transformation of the soul in God by love which is only then accomplished when there subsists the likeness which love begets.' This super-natural union (which St John of the Cross calls 'the union of likeness') 'takes effect *when two wills, the will of God and the will of the soul, are conformed together*, neither desiring aught repugnant to the other.'[60] A baby, receiving the grace of divine adoption at baptism but not yet able to will at all, equally cannot reject God, as those who are of the age of reason can do.

Distinguishing between the different modes or extents of God's presence, Marie-Eugène[61] says that 'by the presence of immensity [simply,] God fills the soul but resides there as a stranger. To the soul enriched by grace and bringing it into action, however, God gives Himself as a friend and father . . . opens up His intimate life, His life in a Trinity, and has the soul enter to share in it like a true child.' Marie-Eugène adds: 'The spiritual life is a progressive interiorization. Once God is discovered to be in the depth of the soul, all its desire will be directed to Him there. In order to see Him and to find Him, the soul must be orientated and move toward its own depths.' St Teresa of Avila, in *The Way of Perfection*, wrote: 'I should not have left Him alone so often, but should have stayed with Him sometimes and not have kept His dwelling-place in such disorder.'[62]

Increase of Divine Life

The Divine super-natural indwelling in a soul in grace is not static in its effects. The mystics[63] speak of divine grace *dilating* the soul, making it bigger. The soul has no physical dimensions as the body has; this therefore is a metaphor. And both a large goblet and a thimble-glass – each of these – can be full, as Teresa and Thérèse remind us.

Similarly, look at the figures of speech which Elizabeth herself uses[64] to direct attention to the factor of increase, by the will's response to grace; increase of the baptismal life of the soul. The metaphors she uses emphasise that it is not God's life but our capacity for that life which increases: that we can be taken deeper and deeper into the divine infinitude. 'He is there to lift me up again and carry me further into Himself, into the depths of that divine Essence in which we already dwell by grace and where I would like to bury myself so deep-down that nothing could draw me forth from there.'[65] She speaks of God's grace and help as proportioned to our receptivity. 'The good God has an immense desire to enrich us with His graces, but it is we who determine the measure for Him, in the proportion that we know how to let ourselves to be immolated by Him . . .'[66] And, elsewhere: 'He said to one of his saints [St Catherine of Siena] "Your measure will be my measure". So make Him a very large measure.'[67]

Philipon's words, when he writes of progress in the spiritual life, are that participation in the life of the Trinity includes 'every possible shade of the deiform life in souls, from the first steps of the newly-baptized child to the most divine acts of "the earth's rare perfect souls"', as St Thomas Aquinas calls them.[68]

A commentator on Elizabeth, Mother Amabel, of the Rochefort Carmel,[69] draws attention to some words of St John of the Cross on the growth in holiness that is possible. They relate to the extent to which a person in grace is given up to God.

As a fire may be just alive or blazing, so may a person's love for God be. In *The Ascent of Mount Carmel*, referring to those who are in grace, to whom super-natural life has been communicated, St John of the Cross wrote that some, on earth, 'rise to higher degrees of love than others. That soul, therefore, has greater communion with God, which is most advanced in love, that is, whose will is most conformable to the will of God. And that soul which has reached perfect conformity and resemblance is perfectly united with, and supernaturally transformed in, God.'[70]

St John of the Cross, following the Old and New Testaments, uses nuptial metaphors: betrothal and marriage (the latter involving 'personal union and mutual self-surrender').[71] For those who have access to the infinite blessing of the Eucharist, Christ linked the maintenance and increase of supernatural life in us with the Eucharistic, personal, giving of Himself.[72]

Humility and self-esteem

It is not adopting situation-ethics to say that this is a subject on which one has to distinguish between situations. For if one is out of balance as compared with firm and unchanging truth, one's imbalance may be either in one direction or in the very opposite direction.

Persons who are prey to an all-pervasive self-disgust, amounting to despair or near-despair about themselves and the future, positively need to acquire that self-esteem which comes from the realization that as individual human beings they are loved and have been created for a glorious eternal destiny if with God's help they will do what is necessary to attain it. Not to know this is not to know a central truth and thus not to evaluate oneself properly.

But what, we may ask, is the position (in relation to central truth) of one who is, not self-disgusted indeed but self-*satisfied*?

Père de Caussade talked about 'the seducing illusions of self-love'.[73] Chesterton said that if he were asked to preach just one sermon, he would begin by telling people 'not to enjoy themselves'. That phrase, he remarked, would probably be misunderstood. 'I should tell them to enjoy dances and theatres and joy-rides . . . to enjoy jazz and cocktails and night-clubs if they can enjoy nothing better . . . but never learn to enjoy themselves.' Never enjoy *themselves*.[74]

Humility is good and is sane because it is accordance with reality. Pride, by which the self-satisfied or self-worshipping are seized, is not. Chesterton illustrated why this is both so and seen to be so. "'E comes in 'ere and 'e thinks 'e's Gawd Almighty", says the man in the bar. *Au fond*, the reason why such self-glorification provokes a deeply unfavourable reaction from us, the fellow human beings subjected to it, is that it is not in accordance with fact and truth, not in accordance with the 'is-ness' of the self-glorificator.

There is a spectrum of possibilities: from the self that, as we say, is 'full of itself' to the glorious example of the Saint who is so empty of self that he or she is a person 'filled', as it were, with the indwelling God and transformed.

This being Elizabeth's message, as well as that of St John of the Cross, St Teresa and spiritual writers without number, one wonders how an American priest-author[75] can write: 'The entire journey of faith begins and ends with self-love'! What he has in mind, no doubt, is the need to combat self-disgust of which we have spoken above (self-disgust being a dire and unhealthy state, to be distinguished from a self-disapproval and self-distrust that are basically healthy, the opposite of prideful self-satisfaction). If, relying on God and not yourself, you esteem yourself because God loves you and is taking you in hand, that surely is fine, since it is God you are then glorifying, not your own self apart from God.

But the same author in fact mentions St John of the Cross and, quite amazingly, presents the latter's 'self-contempt' as undesirable, as something about which we know so much better today. He actually ascribes it to unfortunate experiences in the Saint's childhood and religious life. But the self for which John of the Cross had contempt was the self self-related, as distinguished from the self united to and dependent on God. John had a deep perception of the nothingness of that self in comparison with God. The 'self-contempt' did not prevent him – indeed it impelled him to – shouting with joy at the fact that the Trinity had stooped down to him, had created him as a loved being for an eternal destiny. 'Really someone' therefore, we may say – of him in the sixteenth century and of us now.

The joyous Elizabeth insisted that we ought to be vessels full of God and empty of *us*. 'If (wrote Elizabeth) He finds my soul empty of all that does not come within these two words: "His love, His glory", then He chooses it to be "His bridal chamber". He rushes there . . .'[76]

'Praise of glory'

Elizabeth had a penchant for using and conferring motto-names. *Janua Coeli*, Gate of Heaven, was the name she chose from the Litany to use when referring to Our Lady: after death 'it will be she . . . who will introduce me to the eternal courts'.[77] *Laudem Gloriae*, 'Praise of Glory', taken from St Paul ('That we may be unto the praise of His glory'[78] – *in laudem gloriae*), was what Elizabeth chose as a name for herself. It expresses what she wanted to do and be.[79] Another nun in the Dijon convent asked Elizabeth to suggest a similar name that she also could use for her constant guidance and inspiration. Elizabeth chose for her *Abscondita*, 'Hidden one',[80] a name which again was taken from St Paul ('your life is hid with Christ in God').[81]

The glory of God and her praise of it. 'There is a double movement in our love for God', writes Philipon. 'To love God for our sake is perfectly legitimate. It is to seek in Him the satisfying term of all our powers . . . [but] St Augustine points out another manner of loving God and seeking after divine union: "To live by God for God's sake"; and St Thomas: "To live not for ourselves but for God". This is the summit and the highest definition of the spiritual life. Not that the love is a disinterested Pure Love that excludes the idea of eternal beatitude which is so sanctifying,[82] but one which loves God for God's sake first, as is right.'[83] Right, and in accordance with reality, for God is not merely lovable but is Lovableness itself. Elizabeth's desire was based on the supreme desirability of God.

That point is worth pausing upon. Would that when we think of 'heaven' we could escape from our customary mind-jerk reaction and could jettison the merely figurative picture of white robes and harps. I doubt whether harps will actually feature in heaven at all. Elizabeth gives us the true picture, or a glimpse of it: 'Adoration . . . it can, I think, be defined as the ecstasy of love. It is love overcome by the beauty, the strength, the immense grandeur of the Object of its love.'[84] 'Would that', cried out St Bernardino to his hearers in the great piazza at Siena, 'would that I might behold you all, and myself along with you, intoxicated with the wine of the glory of life eternal.'

And yet not 'overcome' (*ecrasé*), not crushed, *to nothing*, our individual self: but in a mysterious way transformed, by

Divine adoption: 'we shall be like Him', says St John the Evangelist.[85]

This is what we were made for: it is the intended end and purpose of the journey. We really have got it wrong if we think of it as a mere appendage ('all this, and heaven too'). Even more so if we look around at the tense bustle of the airport and strangely think it is our destination. There is a need not to be taken in by the immediacy and tangibility of the world of bricks and asphalt pavements and computers, of fast food or oysters; even of the sunset over Skiddaw. Insignificant if not trashy, all these, compared with that which our minds cannot now conceive or put a shape to: 'The eye hath not seen, nor ear heard, neither hath it entered into the heart of man, what things God hath prepared for them that love Him.'[86] Even the human love we experience on earth, however passionate and however deep, is (as the hymn says) 'only a shadow'.

In the praise and adoration, here on earth, of the glory of God we simply recognize truth, we sanely act in accordance with its 'is-ness'. That, the glory of God, is how it factually is. It is not how *we* are, apart from God's grace, not how we are of our nature – though, as Chesterton shows us, we often act as though it were otherwise. Attitudes and expressions which are so out of place when used by ourselves in relation to ourselves are not so when used of God (and by God, *of* God), for the gloriousness and the centrality no more than represent what God in fact IS. A soul's 'praise of glory', here and eternally, is a recognition of the fact-ness, the 'is-ness', of God and God's attributes.[87]

Consider, Sheed writes, what the Church sees when she looks at the universe. 'For one thing, She sees all things whatsoever held in existence from moment to moment by nothing but the continuing will of God that they should not cease to be. When She sees anything at all, in the same act She sees God holding it in existence. Do we? It is not merely a matter of knowing that this is so. Do we actually see it so? If we do not, then we are not living mentally in the same world as the Church. What is more, we are not seeing things as they are, for that *is* how they are.'[88]

Outrageous as it may seem to insist on it, the position as expressed by Sheed applies in the case of everyone, including those who would regard what he says as indistinguishable from fairy-tale. Some people almost seem to think that because they personally do not believe in eternity it will not happen for them.[89]

Humility, then, is appropriate in relation to us, glory is appropriate in relation to God, simply because that is the actuality of the situation – we in comparison to God, God in comparison to us. It is simple ontological reality. Therefore, if we are content with *ourselves* (though the Other is attainable and offered to us), we set our sights very low.

Desiring an attainable Prize

Some time soon we shall, individually, leave time and enter eternity – eternity of one sort or another – come what may. Is it not odd for a believing person to be indifferent to that, or to accept it merely notionally and to act as though such a transition were not going to happen? The Penny Catechism speaks of a 'firm trust' that God will give us eternal life, i.e. heaven, 'and all means necessary to obtain it, if we do what he requires of us'.[90] (We repeat that, clearly, God will not 'require' of a person what is not known to that person as a requirement.) The Penny Catechism specifies, also, the two 'sins against Hope', namely despair and, its opposite, presumption. One consoling thought – though it ought not so to operate as to induce presumption and leaving too late our turning back to God after grave and conscious sin – is that until our last breath is drawn we need not despair.

Elizabeth, in tune as she was with the Church, speaks of the hour of death as 'the *decisive* hour', since we shall remain for all eternity in the state in which God finds us, and since (she adds, about those who die in grace) 'the degree of our grace will be the measure of our glory'.[91]

St Bernard wrote that: 'every soul, even if it is loaded down with sins, ensnared in vices, trapped by the enticements of pleasure, a captive in exile . . . enslaved by cares, distracted with business, shrinking with fear, afflicted with griefs . . . can turn back and find that it can not only breathe the hope of forgiveness and mercy, but even dare to aspire to be the Bride of the Word, when it is not afraid to make alliance with God and take on the sweet yoke of love with the King of the angels.'[92]

Given that this involves reliance on God rather than on our own self, it is an antidote to the despair of self-disgust – which is an aberration, no less than is the spiritual disease of self-adoration (which is situated in the region of the opposite pole to despair, that of presumption). The first got out of the way, the second can be tackled.

We are nothing in ourselves and apart from God, but *as beings loved by God* our status is immense. Hence, rightly insisting on our own nothingness is not the same thing as saying that we are of no importance. And though we cannot add in any way to God's essential glory, God's 'is-ness', or to the Trinitarian happiness, we can (in return for God's love for us) give God the gift of love and increase what theologians call His 'accidental' glory.[93] The glory we give Him is proportioned to our holiness: the holiest soul gives Him the most glory. (The larger the vessel has become on earth – that metaphor again – the more it contains and gives back to God in its fullness-to-the-brim in heaven.) One can say, indeed, that it is in proportion to our *happiness* that God finds His accidental glory.

St Augustine's aphorism is well known: 'Thou hast made

us for Thyself, and the heart of man is restless until it finds its rest in Thee'. But consider how, with our innate egocentricity, we tend to home in more on the second part of it – our complete fulfilment in heaven, entirely true as that is – than upon the first part, which is equally true, namely: 'Thou hast made us for Thyself'. We were created *for God's glory*, and our purposed end (as well as our beatitude[94]) is to give God glory.

'Without Me you can do nothing'[95] is absolutely central, but should not be misunderstood.[95a] Possessing free will, we are *not* merely passive canvases waiting to be painted-on so as to be made into works of art by the Divine Artist. We become what the active exercise of our wills makes us to be. But since 'without Me' – without God's grace – one can, literally, 'do *nothing*', we are scarcely in any position to *self*-direct the glory if we achieve and be what God wants us to achieve and to be. An artist works through his medium. God, Divine and creative Artist, works through the medium of the exercise of our free will – the latter active at the same time as it passively consents to be acted-on.

In having eternity always before her, Elizabeth saw things as they are. In her mind, moreover, she did not separate her present existence from the eternal existence to which she was journeying (except as regards the obvious difference between the darkness of faith now and the clarity of vision in eternity). She was resolved to do and be *now*, through her will wholly orientated to God, what it would be her eternal happiness to do and be in heaven. She wrote of time as 'eternity begun, but ever in progress.'[96] Her endless heaven would begin now.

The Church teaches firmly that if someone goes to share in the Beatitude of the Trinity, it is *through Christ*, God-made-man, and the Church, the Mystical Body of Christ, that he or she goes: and that applies even to one who in some remote part of the world, whilst saved through living a good life according to his or her lights, has never heard of Christ,[97] or who in the civilized world has only a fragmentary knowledge of Him.

How beautifully encapsulated is Philipon's description of Christ's preoccupation on earth: 'The soul of Christ was constantly day and night possessed by a twofold yearning: for the redemption of the world and the glory of His Father.' Christ, God-made-Man. 'Equal to His Father as God – "I and the Father are One"[98] – as Man, He shows submission and reverence for Him in His every act.'[99]

Continuous Praise of Glory

Elizabeth's desire to be a 'Praise of glory' was not a limited one, as though she had said 'I will set aside a time every day during which I will live in the presence of God and praise Him'. That would have been a splendid aspiration, and we might think we were doing well in doing as much as that. But it was something continuous, extending to every minute, that Elizabeth sought. Her reasoning was: since God, by His grace, is in my soul, continuously, I can live in heaven beforehand, continuously. In this 'anticipated Heaven',[100] heaven in advance, she would do, by grace and her own efforts, what the blessed in heaven cannot *but* do. With them it is like a torrent, rushing towards the Divine depths. In heaven, as she wrote, 'each soul is a praise of glory to the Father, to the Word, to the Holy Spirit, because each soul is held fast in pure love and "no longer lives by its own life, but by the life of God."'[101]

'How', she wrote, 'can I imitate, within the heaven of my soul this ceaseless occupation of the blessed in the Heaven of glory . . . this praise, this uninterrupted adoration? . . . The soul that penetrates and dwells in these "deep things of God"[102] . . . that consequently does everything "in Him, with Him, by Him and for Him", with that limpidity of gaze

29

which gives it a certain resemblance to the one, simple Being – this soul, by each of its movements, of its aspirations, as well as by each of its acts, however ordinary they may be, "is rooted" more deeply in Him it loves. Everything in it renders homage to the thrice-holy God. It is (so to say) a perpetual *Sanctus*, an unceasing Praise of Glory!'[103]

And, elsewhere: '"Abide in Me."[104] It is the Word of God who gives this command, who expresses this wish. Abide in Me; not for a few moments, a few passing hours, but *abide*, in a permanent, habitual way. Abide in Me, pray in Me, adore in Me, love in Me, suffer in Me, work, act in Me. Abide in Me for your dealings with every person or thing . . .'[105]

'He never leaves you',[106] she said; and she for her part wished '*to love Him all the time*'.[107]

Transformation

The sought transformation, of which Elizabeth constantly speaks, is one related centrally to Christ. '"I live, now not I, but Christ liveth in me": I no longer want "to live by my own life, but to be transformed in Jesus Christ, so that my life may be divine rather than human",[108] and that the Father, in bending over me, may recognize the image of the beloved Son in whom He has placed all His delight.'[109]

What we are now about to glimpse is Elizabeth having ceased to be a spiritually single woman, as it were; and not merely 'dwelling' in her Spouse but being 'transformed in Him', transformed into the gracious image of Christ, through loving surrender of her will. 'Love', wrote St John of the Cross, produces 'such a resemblance by the transformation of those who love that one may be said to be the other, and both but one.' He says the reason is that each 'gives himself up to the other . . . resigns, abandons and exchanges himself for the other.'[110]

A number of aspects of this may be seen in Elizabeth's letters and other writings. One of them is her striking determination to *go out of herself*. She remembers that phrase from an old treatise she has read, which contains the words: 'love . . . carries the lover outside himself into the bosom of the beloved,'[111] ('so as to transport the lover with an ineffable ecstasy into', is how Elizabeth puts it). She adopts this phrase: 'He wants you to go out of yourself, to leave every pre-occupation, in order to retire to that solitude He has chosen for Himself in the depths of your heart.'[112] A paradox: she 'goes out of herself' but the Spouse is in her own heart, and there it is that she goes. God, she wrote, wants you to love and adore Him where He dwells in the soul, to live intimately with Him 'when one knows how to find' Him there.[113]

St Thérèse of Lisieux stated what she thought her mission in heaven would be: 'making God loved as I love Him'. Elizabeth (perhaps in conscious or subconscious imitation of Thérèse) made her own statement: 'It seems to me that in Heaven my mission will be to draw [to attract as a magnet does] souls, in helping them to go out of themselves so as to adhere to God by a wholly simple and wholly loving movement, and to keep them in that great inner silence which allows God to imprint Himself in them . . .'[114]

Her constant desire is to be, not Elizabeth-on-her-own[115] but Elizabeth-with-Christ, transformed in Christ. She wants to be 'so captured by Him' that she can 'no longer go out of His radiance'.[116] Her desire is to dwell in Christ, as He in her, 'at every moment'.[117] Nor are her concerns limited to those of her own personal love-relationship with Him: 'since we are all members of one body, it is in so far as we have divine life abundantly that we shall be able to communicate it' to others.[118]

She wishes to 'adhere' to God, 'gaze' towards God, 'live habitually in' God, 'be rooted' in God, 'surrender herself

31

to' God.[119] 'We look at ourselves too much', she wrote, 'we would like to see and understand, we do not have enough confidence in Him who envelops us with His Charity.'[120] She wishes God, within her, to 'absorb' and 'possess' her.[121] 'I do everything with Him, so I go to everything with a divine joy; whether I'm sweeping or working or at prayer . . .'[122] 'He is in me, I am in Him, I have only to love, to let myself be loved, and that all the time, through all things: to wake in Love, to move in Love, to go to sleep in Love, soul in His soul, heart in His heart, eyes in His eyes, so that by His contact He purifies me, He delivers me from my misery . . .'[123]

She describes herself as a 'broom' to be either used or put by. Whatever may be God's will:

> With my spirit singing I cry:
> 'I have faith in Your love for me!'[124]

By all this we see what is meant by the 'disappearing' Elizabeth, the one who seeks to be wholly 'forgetful' of herself. 'I am "Elizabeth of the Trinity"', she wrote in 1903, 'that is, Elizabeth disappearing, losing herself, letting herself be invaded by the Three.'[125] She quotes Blessed John Ruysbroeck: Christ 'wants to consume our life in order to change it into His own . . . if only we renounce ourselves.'[126]

Abbot Marmion wrote that 'the special effect of the Blessed Eucharist' on a soul which receives this sacrament with the proper dispositions is, 'if I might coin the word . . . to *Christify*'. As he put it, the soul united to Christ loses – not its existence but – 'its separate existence'. 'Through faith, the thoughts of Christ become its thoughts, through love, the desires of Christ become its desires, and by an act of perfect *abandon* its will is entirely subordinated to the will of Christ. It effects so complete a transformation that the soul can say: "I live, now not I, but Christ liveth in me"'.[127]

We recall Christ's words in His Prayer to the Father: '. . . that they also may be one in Us . . . I in them, and Thou in Me' (John 17:21 and 23), and His 'he that eateth my flesh, and drinketh my blood, abideth in me, and I in him' (John 6:57). Marmion wrote of 'the soul's dream: to make only one with the beloved'; Holy Communion, 'in which the soul receives Christ as food, realizes this dream in transforming the soul, little by little, in Christ.'[128]

A most interesting word (one we have already seen used by Thérèse) comes into Elizabeth's pages. It is 'fusion'.[129] The word has an overtone of marriage, of the soul as a spouse. How strange, yet pleasant, that this leads my mind from the language of faith to a detective story. A character of Margery Allingham's remarks, about the state of mind of two human beings intensely in love: 'they're never the same again, are they? A fusion of metals and all that. I mean, love isn't a cement, it's a solvent.' In another detective novel she makes a character say: 'To love is to become molten, you understand, and to pour one's self into a die.'

Yet 'fusion', and phrases of Elizabeth and Marmion about transformation *into* Christ, are surely lovers' exaggeration, situated in the lands between what can and cannot be expressed. They are of the nature of 'It isn't I that now live . . . and yet it is'. St Bernard, who speaks of drops of water mingled with wine, also insists, to avoid misunderstanding, that 'the substance' [the identity of a person as a creature] remains. St John of the Cross, for all his metaphors of coal becoming fire, wrote that the substance of the soul is 'inconvertible' into God (adding, nevertheless, that 'being united to Him and absorbed in Him' the soul can be *'by participation* God').[130]

It is not, then, a question of complete loss of identity. Infused with Divine life, 'transformed and divinized' even,[131] the human person remains and loves.[132]

33

Love through the will

If we are tempted to think of all that as pious rhetoric only, it is as well to bear in mind, first, that essentially one loves God with the will, not the emotions ('If you love me, you will keep my commandments')[133] and, second, that Elizabeth, daily, in every aspect of her life, without reservation, set herself to do the will of God. And that is an accurate description of much more than 'Lord, Lord!'.[134] Actually willing and actually doing are concrete enough, not abstract and theoretical.

Only God, Absolute Truth and Justice, Absolute Love, whose desire it is 'that my own joy may be in you and your joy be complete',[135] but who seeks a free reciprocity from the loved one – only God can both command and beg at the same time.[136] The message of His Church, speaking with His authority, is one of command and exhortation blended.

As for Elizabeth's response: even before she entered Carmel she had written, in her private diary: 'I feel ready to die rather than offend You voluntarily, even by venial sin'; but also, asking pardon, 'I am so imperfect'.[137] Seven years after, in Carmel, she writes that, 'I see the multitude of my negligences, of my faults' (describing herself as 'indigent'),[138] yet 'If, like our adored Master we can say at the end of each day "Because I love my Father, I always do the things that please Him",[139] He will really be able to consume us [like a fire], and like . . . little sparks we shall go on to lose ourselves in the immense blazing Hearth, to burn there at our ease throughout eternity.'[140] 'Loving is so simple', she wrote, 'it is surrendering yourself to all His wishes.'[141]

St Bernard, writing on transforming union, said that when *conformity with the will of God* has reached a certain degree, union of Word and soul takes place. 'The substance will remain, but re-clothed in a new form, the form of God Himself.'[142] Marmion wrote: 'It is by a living faith, the conviction of the Divinity of Jesus Christ, that we live the divine life ... By this faith, we identify ourselves in some way [in a certain manner] with Jesus Christ' in our thoughts, desires, words and actions. 'Then comes to pass the: "I live, now not I, but Christ liveth in me ..."'[143]

Coherence of Elizabeth's thought

We can, then, see how the various strands of Elizabeth's thought we have mentioned above – the Indwelling of the Trinity, 'Disappearance of self', Praise of Glory, Transformation through love and conformity of wills – are not each to be taken in isolation; they intertwine and form a coherent whole. We can see, too, that they are more than merely devotional ideas or musings; they are solidly based on Scripture. They are personal restatements of Christ's own words and those of St Paul.

God's 'abiding' in the soul that is in grace: '. . . *my Father will come to him, and we will . . . make our abode in Him.*' The creature's 'abiding' in God: '*Abide in me: and I in you*': the Divine purpose of this mutual abiding being that the creature, living with the life of Christ, shall give glory to the Triune God and achieve eternal fulfilment through and in so doing. The central fact that we give glory to God in the measure that God's will operates in us: in measure (that is) as, perceiving God's will, we accept it, make it our own and try to act in accordance with it. Further, the remarkable paradox that it is the death of self which produces the enhancement of self. A dying of self in order that a transformed self may live – and, after our days here, live loving and adoring in *clarity*: wonderingly, with soul singing, joyfully overwhelmed by the beauty of the 'You' that is the Trinity.

St Paul's 'I live, now not I'. And as St John the Evangelist expressed it (while pointing out that in what manner this, in heaven, will be is not yet known to us), we shall be '*like to*'[144] God – by '*adoption*', St Paul says elsewhere, as a child is adopted into a family, not by any inherent right of its own but through love on the part of the Adopter.

It is in this sound Scriptural sense, and not in any other, that Elizabeth speaks of 'deification' based on one's personal identification with Christ, God-made-man;

> That He may deify, let us dwell here –
> Our souls in His soul, and our eyes in His.[145]

'Changeless Beauty, that wishes to fascinate us, to captivate us; more than that, to deify us!'[146] We who by nature are nothings ('Who is like to God?') can be made 'like to' Him by grace and participation. Though astounding, it is not *more* astounding that we can become 'like God' than that God should have become 'like us', at the Incarnation.

Our losing is gloriously finding, when the 'grain of wheat dies'.[147] Would that we were more ready to proceed from our forgiven sins and our stupidities, not to self-justification – as though the sins and the stupidities had not really occurred and we could retain our self-complacency, but rather to the blithe throwing-out of that ridiculously stuck-up clown, our self.[148] In her diary, Elizabeth summarized the message she had taken from a retreat: '. . . humble oneself in all things, humble oneself in seeing one's faults, and, instead of holding a grudge against oneself, recognize one's weakness and one's nothingness'; and she added: 'O Mary, to whom I pray daily for humility, come to my aid.'[149]

'Spending' herself for the Beloved

A cell in the Body of Christ, the Church, by baptism, Elizabeth – like Thérèse – sought the fulfilment of her self through the 'mystical death'[150] of that self. 'Its inmost nature is entirely possessed and activated by God', says a writer on St Bernard, of transforming union.[151] In a poem Elizabeth strikingly spoke of the *giving up of ownership of herself*: 'You are no longer yours' [lit. 'you no longer belong to yourself']: in that, she added, was where greatness lay.[152]

Referring to St Paul's 'you are dead; and your life is hid with Christ in God'[153] (which is what Paul desired for his hearers during their life on earth), Elizabeth exclaims: 'That is the condition: it's necessary to be dead![154] Without that one can be hidden in God at certain times; but one does not LIVE habitually in this divine Being, because all the feelings, personal pursuits and the rest, come to draw us away.'[155] She wrote: 'He so thirsts to associate us with all that He is.'[156] And: '. . . we love each other so much!!'[157]

Loss of self in the Beloved, transformation of self into the image of the Beloved – these are inextricably linked in Elizabeth's mind. 'Loss of self' in order to be 'transformed' is a *leitmotif* of Elizabeth's poems, of her writings generally:

I lost in Him, with Him as one . . .[158]

Souls come and merge themselves in such a Love . . .[159]

> To see the Master here
Annihilate His self
> before His Father thus,
Means now that, in our turn,
> *we* want to disappear . . .[160]

Annihilate your self, to find by this
The hidden God your being longs to reach.[161]

Let Elizabeth disappear, let Jesus only remain![162]

It's there that will occur
> the transformation! – there
That I shall, ah, become
> as if another You.[163]

In her Prayer to the Holy Trinity, composed and written down in 1904, she asks Christ to 'substitute Yourself for me': 'O my beloved Christ . . . I ask You to "clothe me with Yourself", to identify my soul with all the movements of Your soul, to submerge me, to invade me, to substitute Yourself for me, so that my life may be but a radiance of Your Life'.

Quoting repeatedly St Paul's words, that Christ 'loved me, and gave Himself for me',[164] she sought to deliver up herself completely in return: 'when I see how *He* gave Himself up for me, it seems to me that *I* can do no less for *Him* than spend myself, wear myself out, in order to give Him back a little of what He has given me!'[165] She desired that her will be entirely lost in the will of God.[166] Marmion described such a state (pp. 124–125 of the present book): 'Given up to love, the soul no longer has anything of her own, nor does she live any more for herself; she belongs wholly and entirely to her Beloved.'

In a letter the day after her twenty-first birthday Elizabeth had written: 'Let us go to Him who wants us to be wholly His . . .'[167]

Suffering

It is a truly big thing when (beforehand, and if it comes) we are willing to accept – and, in accepting it, to put to good use – any suffering which God may possibly permit to come our way. But we are taken aback when we read of the saints positively *desiring* that suffering shall come their way. Are they masochists? No. They do not take pleasure in suffering and pain in itself.[168] They have at least three admirable motives for their desire, which have been summarized by a writer on St Thérèse of Lisieux: 'She [Thérèse] had a great desire for suffering because she considered it the supreme proof of love, as the most adequate way of becoming identified with the divine Saviour, and the best means of realizing God's will to save . . . souls' (Abbé Combes).[169]

In Elizabeth, as in Thérèse, we see this exemplified to the letter. It is certain that she had a positive desire to suffer. Her motives, like those of the Saint of Lisieux, were a humble and reciprocal identification with Christ who suffered for us; a deep love for Him which her own acceptance (and more than acceptance) of suffering would demonstrate; and co-operation with Christ in His redemptive work as urged by St Paul – these emerge repeatedly from her writings. 'If we knew how to appreciate the happiness of suffering', she wrote, 'we would be ravenous for it: consider, thanks to it we are able to give something to God . . .'[170] (It was not an academic opinion; she wrote this in the midst of her own physical sufferings.)

And: 'The Master called the hour of His Passion "His Hour" . . . When a great suffering or a really small sacrifice presents itself to us, oh, let us think very quickly that it is "our hour", the hour when we are going to prove our love for Him who, as St Paul says, loved us exceedingly.'[171] 'Our affirmation's greater thus', she wrote, about martyrdom.[172] Sacrificial love is generally recognized as the most noble love of all, and Elizabeth saw her sufferings both as conformity with the sufferings of Christ and as productive of spiritual good for others in 'giving Him souls'. (Her motives, primarily Christ-orientated, are inextricably orientated towards others also – for their sake and for His.)

Being conformed to the image of Christ meant for her being conformed to the whole Christ. A Carmelite, she wrote, is one who has '*gazed on the Crucified*' and has 'wanted to give herself' – a victim for souls – 'as He did'.[173]

Elizabeth was not a stigmatic, of course (though she suffered much pain before her early death), but the following words of Fr. Francis Marsden, written about stigmatics, seem completely apposite here: 'We as the Body of Christ [the Mystical Body of Christ, the Church] are called "to make up what is lacking in the sufferings of Christ" (Col. 1:24).[174] We do this through the tribulations we experience in our daily lives and by regular penance. However, certain souls have a special vocation to suffer, in order to bring many graces upon the world, and to convert many souls. This idea of "victim souls" runs contrary to the mentality of our comfort-seeking age. We instinctively recoil at suffering. God's ways are not our ways. In the Mass every day Christ the Victim is offered to the Father. Why should some souls not be called more deeply to explore the "victimhood" of the Redeemer?'[175]

The author of those apposite words then quotes a saying of the recently-beatified Padre Pio that might have come from the very lips of Elizabeth: 'I am suffering and would like to suffer even more. I feel myself consumed and would like to be consumed even more. I wish to live, in order to suffer more and more, because Jesus has made me understand that the sure proof of love is only in suffering . . .'

In her Prayer to the Trinity, Elizabeth begs Christ, the Second Person of the Trinity made truly man in the womb of Mary, to 'enter my soul as Adorer, as Restorer and as Saviour'. This, 'that I may be for Him another humanity in which He renews all His mystery'. In a letter she wrote that Christ 'makes a partner in His suffering' one generous enough to share His Cross; that the suffering should be accepted by one 'as a proof of love from Him who wants her to be like Himself'.[176]

Earlier she had written: 'I will return You love for love, blood for blood. You died for me; well, every day I will die to myself, every day I will endure new sufferings, every day I will bear a new martyrdom, and that for You – for You I love so much!'[177] Desiring to suffer, 'to suffer so much', was in order to 'console' Christ, to 'bring back souls' to Him, to 'prove' her love for Him.[178] 'I am avid', she said, 'for sacrifices'.[179]

As she *meant* this, it can be said to have been no ordinary love. It is awesome. *'Oh, Madame, we love one another!'*

She was human, Elizabeth!

If ever, reading Elizabeth's sublime writings, we are misguided enough to think of her as a seraph gliding through the cloisters and not really comparable to us in our lives of temptation, failure and struggle, we can bring to mind some revealing vignettes which appear in passing, here and there. As when, eighteen months before she entered Carmel, she wrote: 'It seems to me that when I receive an unjust comment I feel the blood boil in my veins; all my being revolts!'[180] I treasure, too, the down-to-earth wording of a letter she wrote several months after entry. It was to a friend, about seven years younger than herself, called Françoise but nicknamed by Elizabeth 'Framboise', 'Raspberry'. In this letter from the convent to 'Ma chère petite Framboise', Elizabeth rather lets her young friend have it. 'I see that my Framboise is hardly converted. . . . In the past I have overlooked those fits of temper, but you are no longer a baby now and these scenes are ridiculous . . .' Going on to give sympathetic advice to her, Elizabeth says that as, 'my dear, you have my nature, I know what you are able to do.'[181]

In another letter to Framboise she writes: 'You say I have neither worries nor sufferings [in the convent]. It's true that I am really happy, but if you only knew how even when one is crossed one can be just as happy; one has always to keep one's eyes on the good God. At the beginning one has to make an effort when one feels oneself simply boiling inside; but quite gently, by dint of patience and with the good God, one gets there in the end.'[182]

. . . . . .

41

Like Thérèse, Elizabeth wrote poems – more of them, indeed, than Thérèse did (though many of them are juvenilia and slight). I have translated twenty of her poems as in this book. They are the twenty which appeared in the *Souvenirs*; the edition I have is that of 1913, and the Dijon Carmel have kindly sent me the texts of poems which appeared in other editions. These twenty are very representative of Elizabeth's thought: it was no doubt for this reason that they were selected for that first introduction of Elizabeth to a general readership.

The metrical and other principles I have used in translating are the same as those used for my translations of Thérèse's poems.[183] (As well as Elizabeth's rhyming-schemes, I have reproduced the numbers of syllables in the French lines, though with one general exception. Elizabeth sometimes alternates her line-endings as between 'masculine' and 'feminine', the final vowels of the latter being intended to be sounded as separate syllables. However, in English translation I have throughout confined myself to the former.) But whereas I gave Thérèse's poems in chronological order of their composition, the translations of Elizabeth's poems are here arranged according to their subject-matter and in relation to the passages from Marmion which accompany them.

The introduction to Elizabeth given by this book may prompt the reader to seek out the whole of her writings. I do indeed urge the obtaining of the English translations published by ICS Publications, Washington DC. Those books contain treasure. The separately-published (1984) Volume One of the Complete Works is sub-titled *Major Spiritual Writings*. Volume Two (1995) contains the *Letters from Carmel*. Both, happily, are in permanent print, and Volume Three, which will be devoted to Elizabeth's Diary, Personal Notes, Letters of her Youth and Poems, is in preparation. The complete text of Elizabeth's works in the original French is available: *Elisabeth de la Trinité, Œuvres Complètes* (Les Editions du Cerf, Paris, 1991).

Blessed Columba Marmion

Each of the twenty translated poems has following it a quotation from this remarkable Benedictine writer (whom Rome declared 'Venerable' on 28 June, 1999, and who was beatified on 3 September, 2000). Dom Columba Marmion was the Abbot of Maredsous, Belgium, and wrote generally in French, but he was born in Dublin, the son of William Marmion of Kildare and his French wife. Dom Columba's sixty-five years contain within them Elizabeth's shorter life-span, twenty-six years. He was twenty-two when Elizabeth was born; he died a little over sixteen years after her, in 1923.

That Elizabeth's words and Marmion's are brought together in this book is simply because around the same time I happened to be reading both and was struck by how much in accord their respective words are. Since both were saintly persons who knew the mind of their Mother, the Catholic Church, the similarity of thought is doubtless not surprising. But one does find remarkably close similarities. Which of the two was it who wrote the following: '. . . acting in such a way that the whole of our life may consist of a perpetual *Gloria Patri*'?[184] Well, it was Marmion actually, though one would rightly say it was quintessential 'Elizabeth', so much might those very words have come from her mouth or pen.

One is prompted to wonder whether either had read any writings of the other. Certainly Elizabeth did not read any of Marmion's printed works, for the first of them was published eleven years after her death. Did Marmion read anything of Elizabeth's?

Not, it would seem, by the time he wrote the words quoted above, for they come from a Note of his written at Louvain on 20 January, 1906. This was *some nine months before* Elizabeth's death (9 November, 1906) and the customary sending-out of her obituary circular by Dijon to their sister-Carmels of France. The first publication of the

Souvenirs was over two years after that. (Marmion was Spiritual Director of the Carmel of Louvain, in Belgium, but I know of no specific evidence of contact between the Carmels of Dijon and Louvain during Elizabeth's lifetime; even the obituary circular, Dijon say, would not have been sent to Carmels outside France.[185]) There is no record that the Dijon Carmel was among the numerous convents at which Marmion gave retreats.

But how interesting a coincidence that it was in 1906, the year of Elizabeth's death, that Marmion began the deep study of the doctrine of the Trinity which culminated in his Prayer of Consecration to the Blessed Trinity at Christmas 1908.[186] His Note of 20 January, 1906 begins: 'I have received a strong interior light on the manner of honouring the Blessed Trinity ...'. Dom Raymund Thibaut, Marmion's early biographer, and collator of notes of Marmion's conferences, which form the basis of the latter's books, says that when Marmion speaks of such 'lights' in his various notes he may mean either 'the natural outcome of his own meditations' or, 'and this, as cannot be doubted is the most frequent case, for they bear the impress of their origin . . . inspirations coming down from the Father of Lights from Whom is every perfect gift.'[187]

Up to Elizabeth's death, then, and before the publication of the *Souvenirs*, the presumption from the dates must be of two parallel but separate streams of thought, Marmion's and Elizabeth's.

In the period following the publication of the *Souvenirs* (1909) it is clear that Marmion had indeed come to know of Elizabeth and her thoughts, whether exclusively from the *Souvenirs* or from some other source also. At the top of a page of his private Notebook for 1911–12 he wrote the words 'Sr Elisabeth de la S. Trinité', adding to that, in French also, the following: '. . . Faith is the Face-to-Face in darkness, a possessing in the state of obscurity' St J of the

Cross (pg 134).' This quotation is to be found in the *Souvenirs*,[188] and the page-number Marmion gives shows it to be likely that he took it from the 1910 edition; the pagination of the first edition of 1909 is different.

There is a letter of August 1919 from Marmion to the Sub-Prioress of the Dijon Carmel. She had evidently written to him expressing appreciation of something of his (almost certainly *Christ in His Mysteries*, 1919; possibly *Christ, the Life of the Soul*, 1917). She must have mentioned Sister Elizabeth, for Marmion wrote this in reply:

> I already know of Elizabeth of the Blessed Trinity. Having been the director of a convent for ten years, I know something of the spirit of their glorious Mother [St Teresa of Avila] and I read with great advantage to my soul the lives of her daughters. This holy soul, Sister Elizabeth, understood the mystery of Our Lord. She learnt it in the school of the great St Paul, and the Holy Spirit filled her soul with admirable lights for penetrating into the divine obscurity of the Holy of Holies.

Three years after this, a Belgian cardinal, the celebrated Cardinal Mercier (to whom Marmion was confessor), whilst on his way home from Rome after the canonisation of Joan of Arc, made a pilgrimage to the Dijon Carmel and there remarked upon Elizabeth's holiness. Mercier often used the *Souvenirs* as his bedside reading and warmly recommended the book to his clergy.[189]

We might therefore say that there is a possibility, at least, that Marmion took the flow of Elizabeth's thought into the waters of his own thinking: waters which, before Elizabeth's death and the publication of the *Souvenirs*, had flowed separately but in a parallel course to hers.

With the exception of the two short extracts from letters on p. 199 and two quotations in this Introduction (p. 32), the passages from Marmion in these pages are my own translations from the French, done specially for the book, as are all the quotations from Elizabeth.

Given Elizabeth and given Marmion, the beginning of the twentieth century may be said to have been a period which saw quite a little renascence of Catholic writing on the Blessed Trinity considered not as a proposition of theology only, but as the Source, direct and intimate, of one's personal sanctification and fulfilment. Perhaps a catalyst for such writings was Leo XIII's encyclical *Divinum illud munus*, to which reference has been made. Marmion certainly read it, as one would expect.[190] The name of this encyclical is not well-known today. A few years after the death of Marmion, Dom Louismet published his own small 'treatise on the ecstatic contemplation of the Blessed Trinity', *The Burning Bush*.[191] It was intended to be 'a practical introduction to the art of dealing lovingly with God in the secret of one's own heart'.

Philipon, to whom I have here referred so often, and who wrote *The Spiritual Doctrine of Elizabeth of the Trinity* and *The Spiritual Doctrine of Dom Marmion*[192] – an intriguing similarity of titles in itself – was (as Thibaut puts it) of the view 'that Dom Marmion ranked with Sister Elizabeth of the Trinity and St Thérèse of Lisieux as a teacher designed by Providence to re-establish in our times some of the most fundamental themes of the Gospel'.[193] Elizabeth and Marmion give emphasis to different aspects of the same picture. Each supplements the other with their added illumination. Marmion gives less emphasis than she to the Divine indwelling: and as Philipon notes,[194] what Marmion, studying the first chapter of Ephesians is most seized by – that chapter with its 'praise of glory' which so gripped Elizabeth – is the wonder of God the Father's 'adoption of children through Jesus Christ unto Himself'. Recall, too, Marmion's eloquent words on transformation through the Eucharist (page 32 above).

On the Feast of the Presentation, 1904, the day on which the whole community at the Dijon Carmel renewed their religious profession, Elizabeth under the impulse of grace, straight off and without correction of any word,[195] composed her Prayer to the Trinity: 'O my God, Trinity whom I adore! Help me to forget myself entirely, that I may establish myself in You . . .' At Christmas 1908, as the culmination of the deep study and meditation which had followed his 'strong interior light on the manner of honouring the Blessed Trinity' nearly three years before, Marmion wrote his Prayer of Consecration to the Trinity: 'O Eternal Father, prostrate in adoration at Your feet we consecrate our whole being to the glory of Your Son Jesus, the Incarnate Word . . .' Both prayers can be found on pages 185–187 of the present book.

Marmion's Prayer of Consecration to the Trinity is shorter than Elizabeth's Prayer to the Trinity, but whilst each reflects the individual perceptions of the holy person writing it, the two formulations have elements gloriously in common. **Elizabeth:** '. . . wholly yielded up to Your creative Action'. **Marmion:** '. . . submit to Him our souls, our hearts, our bodies, and may nothing within us move without His orders, without His inspiration'. **Elizabeth:** '. . . that I may establish myself in You'. **Marmion:** '. . . ever carry, like blazing flames, our thoughts, our affections, our actions *on high*, to within the bosom of the Father'. **Elizabeth:** 'O consuming Fire, Spirit of Love, "come down upon me", that there be brought about in my soul a kind of incarnation of the Word . . .' **Marmion:** 'O Holy Spirit, love of the Father and the Son, establish Yourself like a furnace of love in the centre of our hearts.' **Elizabeth:** '. . . that my life may be but a radiance of Your Life.' **Marmion:** 'May our whole life be a "Gloria Patri et Filio et Spiritui Sancto".'

Both these holy persons, surely, wrote under the tutelage

– clear, if obscurely communicated – of the Holy Spirit, Third Person of the Divine Trinity, Spirit of Love and Truth and Wisdom.

Feast of Our Lady of Mount Carmel, 2001

POEMS OF
BLESSED ELIZABETH
OF THE TRINITY

PASSAGES FROM BLESSED
COLUMBA MARMION

1. I PLUNGE IN THE INFINITE

Elizabeth, ill in the infirmary in 1906, wrote this poem for the occasion of the twelfth anniversary of the profession of her Prioress, Mother Germaine. Hence the references in the poem to the 'fêting' of the latter.

In the original, 'Praise of Glory' – Elizabeth's name for herself – appears both in French and in Latin.

> My vessel at its will
> > went out, on open sea
> A gentle glide! Immense
> > the ocean bearing me
> ('How fine a journey out
> > this setting-forth has been!').
> How deep the silence was:
> > The night – oh, how serene.
> *All* under Heaven's vault,
> > Mother, was in repose
> As if it heard the Voice
> > Eternal . . . Then, arose –
> Suddenly rose – some waves
> > and those so deep and tall
> The flimsy little skiff
> > vanished beneath their fall . . .
> The Trinity's embrace –
> > opening now! In this
> I found my centre, deep
> > in the divine abyss.
> Not at the water's edge
> > you'll see me now. I dare
> Plunge in the Infinite –
> > my heritage is there.

My soul has its repose
          in that immensity;
It lives there with 'its Three'
          as in eternity.
Listen, and give me joy —
          O Mother, listen well! —
That 'Praise of Glory' may
          the story's ending tell:
Better to fête you's why
          she's entered into God,
And why she wants to live
          in that august abode;
For since that has no change,
          no ending, she began
To contemplate — ah, so
          ineffable a plan:
Your Feast continues till
          the solemn call is giv'n
That 'Laudem Gloriae'
          shall leave this place, for Heav'n;
Then even better where
          (revealed as there shall be
The secret of His Face!)
          the Father I shall see.

Notes

P 115*

24 September 1906

> 'I dare
> Plunge in the Infinite –
> my heritage is there.'

> ' . . . the unfathomable Trinity'
> (Elizabeth, Last Retreat, Sixteenth Day)

'O my God, Trinity Whom I adore, help me to forget myself entirely, so as to establish myself in You, as still and peaceful as if my soul were already in eternity. May nothing be able to trouble my peace or draw me forth from you, O my Unchanging God, but may each minute take me further into the depths of Your Mystery . . .' (Elizabeth, Prayer to the Trinity).

'The Trinity of Persons is not something secondary in God, super-added from outside to the Divine Essence; the Trinity IS God, the three Divine Persons are the one only God. God is essentially these three distinct Persons, the Father, the Son, and the Holy Ghost . . . whenever we name God, we name the Blessed Trinity.' (Louismet, *The Burning Bush*)

'The Father is uncreated: uncreated also is the Son, uncreated the Holy Spirit . . . The Father is eternal: eternal is the Son, eternal is the Holy Spirit . . . and yet not three Gods but one only God.' (Athanasian Creed)

'The Holy Spirit is from the Father and the Son – not made, nor created . . . but proceeding . . . In this Trinity nothing is before or after, nothing greater or smaller, but all three Persons are co-eternal and co-equal to each other.' (*ibid.*)

*This and the other numbers preceded by 'P' refer to the numbering in the *Œuvres Complètes* of Elizabeth. The dates given are those on or for which the poem was written.

'To hold the fulness of the Divine Nature from no one but from oneself is to be God the Father; to hold the fulness of the Divine Nature as communicated from the Father alone is to be God the Son; finally, to hold the fulness of the Divine Nature from both together the Father and the Son is to be the Holy Spirit.' (Louismet)

'... many have erred about this fundamental dogma of our faith, the doctrine of the Most Holy Trinity, for having rashly ventured to scrutinize the depths of the mystery, when they should have been satisfied with believing and adoring.' (Louismet)

BLESSED COLUMBA MARMION: The Holy Trinity

Human reason can demonstrate that there exists a supreme Being, First Cause of every creature, Providence of the world, Sovereign rewarder, Last End of all things. From this rational knowledge and from its manifestation to us of the relationship between creatures and God, there flow for us certain duties towards God and towards our neighbour, duties which together are the foundation of what is called the natural law, and whose observation constitutes natural religion.

But our reason, powerful as it may be, has been able to discover, with certainty, nothing of the inner life of the supreme Being: the Divine life appears to it infinitely distant, in impenetrable solitude: 'Who ... inhabiteth light inaccessible'.[1]

Revelation has come, bringing us its light.

It teaches us that there is, in God, an ineffable paternity. God is Father: that is the fundamental dogma which all the others presuppose, a magnificent dogma which leaves the reason confounded, but delights faith and transports holy souls.

God is Father. Eternally, before ever created light rose upon the world, God begets[2] a Son to whom He communicates His nature, His perfections, His beatitude, His life;

for to beget is to communicate[3] being and life: 'Thou art my Son';[4] 'from the womb, before the day-star, I begot thee'.[5] Thus, life is in God, life communicated by the Father and received by the Son. This Son, in all things like to the Father, is unique: '*the only Son of God*'.[6] He is unique because He has,[7] with the Father, one same and indivisible Divine nature; and the two, though distinct from each other (by reason of their personal properties 'of being Father' and 'of being Son') are united in a powerful and substantial embrace of love, from which proceeds that third Person whom Revelation calls by a mysterious name: the Holy Spirit.

Such, as far as faith is able to know it, is the secret of the inner life of God. The fullness and fruitfulness of that life is the source of the immeasurable bliss which the ineffable society of the three Divine Persons possesses.

And see how God, not in order to add to His plenitude but to enrich other beings by it, will extend, so to speak, His Paternity. This Divine life, so transcendant that only God has the right to live it, this eternal life communicated by the Father to the only Son and, by them, to the Spirit common to them – this life, God decrees creatures shall be called to share. By a transport of love, which has its source in the fullness of the Being and the Good that is God, this life will overflow from the bosom of Divinity to reach and beatify, in elevating them above their nature, beings drawn from nothing. These purely created beings God will ennoble, and make them hear the sweet name of 'children'. By nature, God has only one Son; by love, He will have a multitude of them, without number: this is *the grace of supernatural adoption*.

(*Christ, the Life of the Soul*, Part I, I.i)

---

[1] 1 Tim. 6:16

[2] See Translator's note below.

[3] 'By the gift of a nature that is similar' (Marmion's note)

[4] Psalm 2:7; Hebr. 1:5, 5:5

[5] Psalm 109 (110):3

6   '... the only-begotten Son who is in the bosom of the Father' (John 1:18)
7   'One should say, more strictly, that He *is* with the Father and the Holy
    Spirit one same Divine nature. The lips of us creatures stammer when it
    is a question of such mysteries.' (Marmion's note)

Translator's note: our language inadequate

Marmion very appositely says that human beings 'can only
stammer' when speaking of the Trinity.

Using our human language, which is all the language we have,
we say 'He', singular, when speaking of God (except in a context
referring to and distinguishing between the Three Divine Persons
as Persons, when we might say 'They'). 'He', a singular pronoun
for the Triune God, is the best our human language can do. In one
sense, indeed, it carries the right overtones, for God is *One* God.
But God is one God *in Three Persons*. Yet, if 'He' is inadequate,
'They' is linguistically impossible in speaking of the Triune God:
'not three Gods, but only one God'.

Of course, sometimes a context shows that in saying 'God' or
'He' one is referring to God the Father, as distinct from the other
two Divine Persons.

In thinking about the Trinity one must beware of taking
expressions in the sense they would bear if used of human beings.
For example, 'begets a son', if used of a human being, would
imply that there was a time when the son did not exist, and that
he then came into being. But the time continuum does not apply
to God: God simply IS. God the Son is *'eternally* begotten of the
Father' (Nicene Creed) – 'eternally' connoting no beginning, as
well as no end. 'Beginning' and 'end' have no application to God.
Though the Son 'proceeds from' the Father – and not the Father
from the Son – the Son is eternal God, as the Father is.

Father and Son, though each is eternal and distinct from the
other, are not *two* self-existent Beings: the Son is 'of *one* Being
with the Father'. 'God from God, Light from Light', says the
Nicene Creed, of the eternally-begotten Son. (As to the mode of
this eternal 'begetting', the words of St Gregory Nazianzen are
apt. 'Let the doctrine be honoured silently; it is a great thing for

thee to know the fact; the mode, we cannot admit that even Angels understand . . .'). And the Holy Spirit, a Divine Person distinct from the Father and the Son, is – mysteriously – Love; the eternal and mutual love of the Father for the Son, of the Son for the Father.

Louismet, commentating on Trinitarian doctrine, uses the helpful language of eternal *circularity*: 'The whole Divine life proceeds from God the Father to His Divine Son and returns to Him through Their Holy Spirit: proceeds from Him without going out of Him: returns to Him without having been separated from Him.' 'It is', says the same writer, like a 'fountain which ever springs and ever flows within its own Divine Self.'

That Life is, as it were, extended by 'adoption'. A sharing in that Life is offered *to human beings also*, through the coming of Christ . . .

Opening words of Elizabeth's manuscript of her *Prayer to the Trinity*.

2. I SAW THE STAR

Elizabeth, still a novice in the Dijon Carmel but just accepted for
profession, wrote this poem for Christmas 1902.
    God the Son, made man – 'Splendour of the Father' – is the
Bridegroom.

I saw the star that showed me by its light
The cradle where my baby King would be:
Then, in that calm – that mystery – of night,
It was as though the star turned round at me:
  I heard an Angel's voice, then (how
  It charmed me!) saying 'Comprehend
  This – it is in your soul that now
  The mystery achieves its end;
    God's Son, His Splendour fair,
    Incarnate now, this morn
    In you. With Mary there
    Embrace God, newly-born –
      For . . . yours He is!'

Star-messenger! This God whose call I hear –
Isn't it true He calls Himself the Spouse!
What can I give Him in this dawn so clear?
His strength, His gentleness, my heart arouse.

The Angel:

'What is your mission here to be?
To know . . . to *love*! – You've this to do –
To penetrate that mystery
He's come down to reveal to you.
  God's Son, His Splendour fair,
  Incarnate now, this morn

In you. With Mary there
Embrace God, newly-born –
   For . . . yours He is!'

A Spouse He is, His voice inviting me;
'Come!' was His word, and that the first He said:
The shining star of His Epiphany
Gleamed – sudden – at the vista's rim ahead.
   Lord, grant my soul its one desire –
   Ah, grant it faith and grant it love;
   And, Spirit! now stir up my fire
   For one-ness with my King above.
      My Hope, my Jesus – oh,
      The Father's Splendour is . . .
      O Word! form me to go
         To You in Bliss.

The Seraph then had gone from earthly sight
But in me, still, his beam was ever such
I, recollected in that gentle light,
By love and faith found God within my touch:
   And, given up to adoration, tried
   To listen . . . would almighty Truth give tongue?
   I heard that song within me which inside
   The bosom of Divinity is sung.
      My Hope, my Jesus – oh,
      The Father's Splendour is . . .
      Look on me! may I go
         To You in Bliss.

God, newly-born: another version has 'your Loved One'.

Notes

P 86

Christmas 1902

> 'I heard that song within me which inside
> The bosom of Divinity is sung.'

The eternal Sonship of the Second Person of the Trinity.
The Three Divine Persons are co-eternal, co-equal.

> '*I am who am*, says God to Moses, speaking to him from amidst
> the flames of the burning bush ... The Bush represents God
> the Father; the bright flame which shoots forth from it without
> separating itself from it, represents the Divine Word [the Son];
> and finally, the heat which emanates at the same time from the
> bush and the flame, aptly represents the Spirit of Love.'
>
> (Louismet)

'The reverential spirit in which the Fathers (of the early Church)
held the doctrine of the *gennesis* [the eternal begetting of the Son]
led them to the use of ... forms of expression, partly taken from
Scripture, partly not, with a view of signifying the fact of the
Son's full participation in the divinity of Him who is His Father
... Such were the images of the sun and its radiance, the fountain
and the stream, the root and its shoots, a body and its exhalation
[breath], fire and the fire kindled from it; all which were used as
emblems of the sacred mystery in those points in which it was
declared in Scripture, viz. the mystery of the Son's being from the
Father and, as such, partaker in His Divine perfections. The first
of these is found in the first chapter of the Epistle to the Hebrews,
where our Lord is called "the brightness of God's glory"'
(Newman).

'That which proceeds from God [the eternal Son] is called at once
God, and the Son of God, and Both are One.' (Tertullian)

The Incarnation, in the womb of Mary. *Though God the Son had no beginning, the Incarnation – God the Son becoming man – was an event in the time-continuum that is our habitat as created beings on earth. From our perspective in time, there were aeons when God the Son was not incarnate, had not taken flesh, and then – at the Annunciation at Nazareth – He took flesh, truly becoming a man, born on the first Christmas Day.*

'Our Lord Jesus Christ the Son of God is God and man. He is God, begotten before all ages, of the substance of the Father, and He is man, born in time of the substance of His Mother: perfect God and perfect man, made up of a rational soul and human flesh, equal to the Father in the Godhead, inferior to the Father in His humanity, who, although God and Man, is not two but one only Christ . . .' (Athanasian Creed).

BLESSED COLUMBA MARMION: The wondrous fact of the Incarnation.

'In the beginning was the Word, and the Word was with God, and the Word was God . . . And the Word was made flesh, and dwelt among us.'[1]

Christ is the Incarnate Word. Revelation teaches us that the Second Person of the Holy Trinity, the Word, the Son, took on a human nature, to unite Himself to it personally. This is the mystery of the Incarnation.

Let us pause a few moments to consider this dogma – at once unprecedented and touching – of a Man-God. This is the fundamental mystery on which all the mysteries of Jesus rest. Their beauty, their splendour, their virtue, their force, their worth derive from this ineffable union of humanity and divinity. We shall not really understand them unless we have in the first place considered this mystery in itself and in the general consequences that flow from it. Jesus is God and man; if we want to know Him as a person, to share His interior states, we must make the effort to understand not

61

only that He is the Word, but also that this Word is made flesh. If we want to honour Him fittingly, it is as necessary for us to recognize the reality of His human nature as it is to adore the divinity to which this nature is united.

What does faith tell us is to be found in Christ?

Two natures, the human nature and the divine nature: Christ is both perfect God and perfect man. Moreover, these two natures are united in so close a way that there is but one person, that of the divine Word in whom the humanity subsists. From this ineffable union results the infinite value of the acts of Jesus, of His interior states, of His mysteries.

(Christ in His Mysteries, IV)

¹ John 1:1, 14

+ Pax
Louvain
21 Décembre [1908]

O Père Éternel prosternés en humble
adoration à Vos pieds nous consacrons
tout notre être à la gloire de Votre
fils Jésus. le Verbe Incarné.
Vous l'avez constitué roi de nos
âmes, soumettez-lui nos âmes. nos
coeurs, nos corps, afin que rien en nous
ne se meuve sans Ses ordres. sans
son inspiration. Qu'unis à Lui nous
soyons portés dans votre sein, et
Consommés dans l'unité de votre
amour.

O Jésus unissez-nous à vous
dans votre vie toute sainte toute

Opening words of Marmion's manuscript of his *Prayer of
Consecration to the Trinity.*

3. THERE IS THIS ONE WHO KNOWS ALL MYSTERIES

Elizabeth wrote this poem for Christmas, 1903. It expresses her response to Christ, born on the first Christmas night, and her thoughts turn to the stupendous event of the Annunciation, nine months before.

'Amo Christum' – 'I love Christ'.

There is this One who knows all mysteries
And who embraced them from Eternity:
And this same One . . . the Father's *Word* He is –
Splendour, that Word, of His Divinity.
  See that One come, with Love's excess,
  With Charity so urgent! Say:
  'Son of the Father's tenderness –
  God gives us Him on this great day.'
    O Word! may – lifelong now –
    I listen to You! so
    Possessed by You, that *how*
    To love be all I know.
    'Amo Christum'.

In me, a house that God is living at,
This Jesus Christ, Divine Adorer there,
Takes me to souls, as to the Father: that
Being the double movement of His prayer.
  Co-Saviour with my Master, here! –
  Whose call to me still drives me on;
  For this, I ought to disappear –
  I lost in Him, with Him as one . . .
    One, Word of Life, with You
    For always! and, above,

Your virgin *host* anew
All shining forth with love.
    'Amo Christum'.

His sanctuary, I! He rests in me –
There is the peace one looks for and attains:
In silence and in deepest mystery,
He's captured me: for ever I'm in chains.
    Ah, to Your ev'ry word to cling,
    Calm in the faith I'm anchored to;
    Adoring You, through everything
    As one who only lives by You!
        Beneath Your splendent Light,
        O Word, by night and day
        May I be now – outright –
        To Your great love, a prey.
            'Amo Christum'.

Mother of God, tell me your mystery;
Of how your earthly life was spent: the way –
Right from the time of 'Fiat' – how you'd be
Buried in adoration, Mary! Say
    How – in a peace, a silence – you
    (What mystery!) could enter in
    To Deeps that none but you could do –
    Bearing the gift of God within.
        Secure in God's embrace
        Keep me, I ask. In me
        His imprint may He place –
        For wholly Love is He.
            'Amo Christum'.

---

lives by You: the metaphor is one of sustenance or food.

Notes

P 88

Christmas 1903

> 'See that One come, with Love's excess ...'

'I like it so much when I think it is for Him I have left everything. It is so good to give when one loves, and I love Him so much, this God who is jealous to have me all for Himself. I feel so much love upon my soul, it is like a Ocean in which I plunge, in which I lose myself: it is my vision on earth while awaiting the face-to-face in light.' (Elizabeth, letter to Canon Angles, around the end of August 1903).

BLESSED COLUMBA MARMION: The Son, Splendour of the Father, became man.

Realized in Adam from the dawn of creation, then crossed by the sin of the head of humankind who drew the whole of his race with him into his disgrace, this decree of love would be restored by a marvellous invention of justice and mercy, of wisdom and goodness. See how the only Son, who lives eternally in the bosom of the Father, unites himself to a human nature, within time; but in so close a way that this nature, while being perfect in itself, belongs entirely to the Divine Person to whom it is united. The Divine life, communicated in its fullness to this humanity, makes it the Son of God's own humanity: this is the admirable work of *the Incarnation*. It is true to say of this man, called Jesus Christ, that He is God's own Son.

But this Son who, by nature, is the only Son of the eternal Father appears here below simply to become the first-born of all those who would receive Him, after having been ransomed by Him: 'the first-born amongst many brethren'.[1] Only-begotten of the Father in the eternal

66

splendours, only Son by right, he is constituted the Head of a multitude of brothers, to whom, by His work of redemption, He will restore the grace of divine life.

And this, in such a way that the same Divine life which derives from the Father in the Son, which flows from the Son into the humanity of Jesus, will circulate, through Christ, into all those who shall be willing to accept Him; it will draw them up to the beatifying bosom of the Father, where Christ has gone before us,[2] after having, for us here below, paid off by His blood the price of such a gift.

All holiness from then on will consist in receiving the Divine life from and by Christ who possesses the fullness of it and who is established as our only Mediator; to preserve it, to increase it constantly, by an adherence ever more perfect, by a union ever more close with Him who is the source of it.

Holiness, then, is a *mystery of divine life communicated and received*: communicated, in God, from the Father to the Son, by an indescribable 'generation'[3] – communicated, outside of God, by the Son to the humanity to which He unites Himself personally in the Incarnation; then, through that humanity, restored to souls ...

When, in prayer, the soul considers this munificence, and these attentions of which it is the object gratuitously on the part of God, it feels a need to lose itself in adoration and to sing grateful praises to the Infinite Being who abases Himself before it to give it the name of 'child'.

(*Christ, the Life of the Soul*, Part I, I.i)

---

[1]   Rom. 8:29

[2]   'I ascend to my Father and to your Father ...'; 'In my Father's house there are many mansions ... I go to prepare a place for you' (John 20:17; 14:2)

[3]   Isaiah 53:8

4. IT IS MIDNIGHT

Elizabeth wrote this poem for Christmas, 1905. It is written first in the persona of one who, having been awaiting the Messiah, greets His coming on the first Christmas Night with joy. But it casts the mind forward to the Crucifixion.

It is midnight, nature is stilled.
All calm, but you hear – like a sigh
Out of souls that are longing-filled
Entreaty, ascending on high
For the One who will freedom bring –
These cries from the waiting are torn.
Of a sudden, the Heavens sing:
'This night the Redeemer is born!'

Refrain
He comes to us! Then, sing Noel,
For He is ours, Emmanuel!

We see this little child, and see
The God who is 'Invisible' –
O mystery, unknowable!
Strong one! almighty Deity;
God hidden, Inaccessible –
Ours now, this little child we *see*!

Of the mystery, David saw
What then, in a psalm, he conveyed:
'The Father's Begotten, before
The first star-of-morning was made.
His pavilion He set on high,

In the sun, in the light above;
No person on earth can fly
From His kindly action of love!'

Refrain
He comes to us! Then, sing Noel,
For He is ours, Emmanuel!

He has as name 'Adorable' –
Rightly – one hears it bending low;
'Faithful' and 'True' – *our Spouse*! Not all
By this we say about Him, though:
'Beginning', He, and 'End'. These are,
As titles, more amazing yet.
Before the dawn, this Shining Star
Whose splendency will never set.

Refrain
He comes to us! Then, sing Noel,
For He is ours, Emmanuel!

I'd like to follow Paul in this:
'*All*, for His love, I've thrown away –
My soul desires one thing, it is
To love Him – more and more each day.
I wish that, understanding more
My Christ and my Redeemer, I
May be a mirror-self before
This One who came to sanctify.'

Refrain
In Carmel, He is life for me,
He is my life. My Heaven, He!

Jesus, who left his Godhead-home
When down to us on earth He sped,
Addressed the Father thus: 'I come
To do Your will' – these words He said.
With God, this Priest-and-Victim, *we* –
Let us make our oblation too:
So intimate our part will be
In what He came on earth to do.

Co-mediators, in support
Of our sweet Saviour – let us now
Restore to Him (by how we've fought)
Befitting honour! This is how:
To give the Father what will be
His glory, so immensely great,
Ourselves an immolation, we
In silence here, should immolate.

In His charity's urgency
Is the Lamb self-giving anew.
'Spring up in your joy' as you see
That the Bridegroom comes into view!
Listen now, for His solemn call
Rings out in the blue of the sky:
'Together (said to us all)
To the Banquet of God, on high!'

Notes

P 96

Christmas 1905

'God, this Priest-and-Victim . . .'
(Elizabeth)

You wished to be
My heart's delight, and came . . . to *die*: Your will
The shedding of Your blood – what mystery! . . .
You're living for me, on the altar still.
(St Thérèse, Poem 32 (21); PN 23)

BLESSED COLUMBA MARMION: The Incarnation at Nazareth, and the Sacrifice on Calvary.

But note well that, on the cross, Christ completed His sacrifice . . .

Christ Jesus, at the moment of the Incarnation, embraced in a single glance everything He was to suffer for the salvation of the human race, from the cradle to the cross, and He devoted Himself from then on to the full accomplishment of the eternal decree: at that moment Jesus made a voluntary offering of His own body to be immolated. Listen to St Paul: Christ 'when He cometh into the world' said to His Father: '. . . behold, I come to do Thy will, O God.'[1] And having thus begun the work of His priesthood by the perfect acceptance of everything willed by the Father and the oblation of Himself, Christ consummated His sacrifice on the cross by a bloody death. He inaugurated His passion in renewing the total gift He had made at the moment of the Incarnation. 'Father', He says when He sees the cup of sorrows He is presented with, 'not my will, but Thine be done':[2] and His last words before expiring will be to say that He has fulfilled it all: 'It is consummated.'[3]

Consider this sacrifice for a little while, and you will see that Christ has carried out the sublimest of acts and

71

rendered to God His Father the most perfect homage. The priest? – it is He, the Man-God, the beloved Son. True, it is in His human nature that He offered this sacrifice, since only a man is able to die. True, also, that this oblation was limited to its historical duration. But the priest who offers is a Divine Person, and this dignity imparts to the immolation an infinite worth. The victim is holy, pure, immaculate, for it is Christ Himself: it is He, the Lamb without stain, who effaces the sins of the world with His own blood, shed to the last drop as in the holocausts. Christ was immolated in our stead, He substituted Himself for us; laden with all our iniquities, He became a victim for our sins: 'the Lord hath laid on him the iniquity of us all.'[4] Lastly, Christ accepted and offered this sacrifice with a liberty full of love: He laid down His own life because He willed to do so;[5] and He willed it solely because He loved His Father: 'that the world may know that I love the Father ... so do I'[6] ...

The death of Jesus ransoms us, reconciles us with God, re-establishes the covenant from which every good thing flows for us; re-opens for us the gates of heaven, restores to us the inheritance of eternal life. This sacrifice thenceforth suffices for everything: this is why, when Christ dies, the veil of the temple of Israel is rent in twain, to show us that the former sacrifices are abolished for ever and replaced by the one-and-only sacrifice worthy of God. 'For by *one* oblation', says St Paul, Christ 'hath perfected *for ever* them that are sanctified'.[7]

Do not be surprised that I have spoken at such length about the sacrifice of Calvary [in a section headed 'The Eucharistic Sacrifice']: this immolation is reproduced on the altar; the sacrifice of the Mass is the same as that of the cross ...

(*Christ, the Life of the Soul*, Part II, VII.ii–iii)

---

[1] Hebr. 10:5, 9
[2] Luke 22:42
[3] John 19:30
[4] Isaiah 53:6
[5] See John 10:18
[6] John 14:31
[7] Hebr. 10:14

Elizabeth's crucifix

5. TO RE-ESTABLISH ALL THINGS IN CHRIST

Elizabeth wrote this meditation on St Paul's words for Mother Germaine, for the occasion of the feast-day of St Germain, the prioress's name saint, in 1904.

The Encyclical referred to is the first by Pope (St) Pius X after his election as Pope the preceding year: 'We declare that our sole aim in the exercise of the Supreme Pontificate is *to re-establish everything in Christ*, so that *Christ may be all in all* . . .'

> The Sovereign Pontiff's words
>   (you'll have them in your mind) –
> In his Encyclical,
>   so beautiful in this –
> Now, like a mystic flower
>   which in my heart I find,
> I offer you today
>   that great desire of his.
> Ah, yes! I truly dream
>   that realized in me
> The gentle Pastor's wish
>   completely may come true:
> In this divine desire
>   my motto is to be
> My Saviour, Christ, 'Restore
>   Ev'rything now, in You'.
>
> So beautiful a plan
>   came straight from God. It came
> From Wisdom's mind itself
>   in His eternity:

The writing of St Paul
      say, ceaselessly, the same —
God's 'overflowing love';
      excess of Charity.
Let's hear those words of Paul;
      simply so we ensure
We hear the high decree
      let us awhile be still:
'That in His presence we
      be holy, we be pure,
God-chosen in Him — we,
      by an eternal Will.'

But also, we have sinned —
      how wretched are we thus!
What comes of us if God
      comes not to grant release?
But, 'rich in mercy', He
      is Father yet for us —
For, know: the prayer of Christ
      doth all His wrath appease.
'To blaze and radiate
      the glory of His grace,
Christ — His redeeming death —
      has justified us': this
Means now that we can see
      the radiance of His face,
For, now, 'adopted sons'
      our high description is.

That so God's Will Supreme
          may be accomplished, say:
'Let us restore in Christ
          the earth, the heavens too':
For heaven is in us
          and thus the Spirit may,
In ardour of His Fire
          that heav'n in us renew.
And let us then restore
          the kingdom, here in France:
Offer 'the Just Man's Blood' –
          this we are ransomed by!
Through Him we shall obtain
          peace and deliverance;
'Pardon' for us, the word
          God will pronounce on high.

'I sanctify Myself
          for them, O Father' – there
You have from Jesus Christ
          His final song of love!
The very source of Life,
          let's recollect that prayer
To make it, night and day,
          rise up to God above.
At that decisive hour
          when all the world must fade
I hope I can repeat
          the Spouse's prayer – I too –

And say: 'I've made You known
          as You desired. I've made
You loved. Your work I've done.
    O God, I come to You!'

'He's brought us out of shades
          of death: on us He dowers
His kingdom-without-end'
          (Paul tells us). He has giv'n
The heirdom of the Saints –
          that heritage is ours:
So we (and even now)
          are citizens of Heav'n.
Yes! such our greatness is:
          such our nobility!
For 'we are Christ's, and Christ,
          the Father's'. For His grace –
For His stupendous Love,
          oh, bless Him ceaselessly!
Our praise of Him ring forth
          in every time and place.

Elizabeth quotes, sometimes in free poetic form, phrases in the first two chapters of
Ephesians; the Gospels of St Matthew and St John; Colossians and 1 Corinthians.

Notes

P 89

15 June 1904

> 'My Saviour, Christ, "Restore
> Ev'rything now, in You".'

'*Instaurare omnia in Christo*. Again it is St Paul who instructs me, St Paul who has just been immersed in the great intentions of God, and who tells me that God has resolved in Himself "to re-establish all things in Christ". In order that I personally may effect this divine plan, see how it is again St Paul who comes to my aid and who will himself trace out a rule of life. "Walk in Jesus Christ", he says to me, "be rooted in Him and built up in Him and confirmed in the faith, and growing more and more in Him through thanksgiving" [*see* Col. 2:6–7]. *To walk in Jesus Christ*. It seems to me that this is to go out of self, to lose self from view, to leave self, in order to enter more deeply in Him each minute that passes: so deeply that one might be rooted there . . .' (Elizabeth, *Last Retreat*, Thirteenth Day).

'O consuming Fire, Spirit of Love, "come down upon me", that there be brought about in my soul a kind of incarnation of the Word: may I be for Him an added humanity in which He renews all His Mystery . . .' (Elizabeth, Prayer to the Trinity).

BLESSED COLUMBA MARMION:
The inheritance restored.

> As you know, it was as far back as the creation of the first man that God effected His design: Adam received, for himself and for his [the human] race, the grace that made him a child of God. But, by his fault, he lost (for himself, as well as for his race) that divine gift . . .
>
> But God, the Church tells us, showed Himself even more wonderful in the restoration of his designs than He had been

at the creation: 'O God, who, in creating human nature, didst wonderfully dignify it, and hast STILL MORE WONDER-FULLY renewed it'.[1] How so? What is this divine marvel? This mystery is *the Incarnation*.

It is through the Incarnate Word that God will restore everything. Such is 'the mystery which hath been hidden from eternity'[2] in the Divine mind and which St Paul comes to reveal to us: Christ, the Man–God, will be our mediator: He it is who will reconcile us with God and give us back grace. And as this great design has been planned from all eternity, it is with reason that St Paul speaks of it to us as an ever-present mystery. It is the last great feature by which the Apostle completes his making the Divine plan known to us.

Let us listen to him with faith, for we touch here the very heart of the Divine work.

The Divine mind is to constitute Christ head of all the ransomed, of every name that can be named in this world and in the ages to come:[3] in order that by Him, with Him and in Him we may all arrive at union with God, that we may achieve the supernatural holiness God asks of us.

No thought could be clearer in the letters of St Paul; there is nothing of which he could be more convinced; nothing he puts in higher relief. Read all his epistles, and you will see that he constantly returns to it, to the extent of making it almost the one substance of his doctrine. See: in this passage from the Epistle to the Ephesians[4] that I quoted to you at the beginning, what is he saying to us? It is '*in Christ*' that God has chosen us, so that we might be holy; He has predestined us to be His adopted sons '*through Jesus Christ . . .*'; we are acceptable in His eyes '*in His beloved Son*'. It is in His Son Jesus that God has resolved to 're-establish all things' or, better, according to the Greek text, to 'bring all things back' under Christ, as under one and only head. Christ is always uppermost in the Divine idea.

How is that effected?

'The Word' – of Whom we adore the eternal generation in the bosom of the Father – 'was made flesh'.[5] The Most Holy Trinity created a humanity like to ours, and from the

79

first instant of its creation united it, in an ineffable and indissoluble manner, to the person of the Word, of the Son, of the Second Person of the Holy Trinity. This God-Man is Jesus Christ. This union is so close that there is only one single person, that of the Word. Perfect God by His divine nature, the Word becomes, by His incarnation, perfect man. In making Himself man, He remains God, "That which was, remained; that which was not, He took to Himself":[6] the fact of having taken a human nature, to unite Himself with it, has not lessened the divinity.

In Christ Jesus, the Incarnate Word, the two natures are united, without mixture or confusion; they remain distinct at the same time as they are united in the unity of the person. Because of the personal character of this union, Christ is God's own Son, He possesses the life of God: 'For as the Father hath life in himself, so He hath given to the Son also to have life in himself.'[7] It is the same Divine life that subsists in God and fills the humanity of Jesus. The Father communicates his life to the Word, to the Son; and the Word communicates it to the humanity that is united to Himself personally. This is why, in looking at Our Lord, the Eternal Father recognizes Him as his true Son: 'Thou art my Son; this day have I begotten thee'.[8] And because He is His Son, because this humanity is the humanity of His Son, it possesses a full and entire communication of all the divine perfections. The soul of Christ is *full* of all the treasures of the knowledge and wisdom of God: 'In whom are hid ALL THE TREASURES of wisdom and knowledge';[9] in Christ, says St Paul, 'dwelleth ALL THE FULNESS of the Godhead corporally';[10] the sacred humanity is 'full of grace and truth'.[11]

The Word made flesh is therefore adorable in His humanity as in His divinity, because under this humanity is veiled the Divine life. O Christ Jesus, Incarnate Word, I prostrate myself before You, because You are the Son of God, equal to Your Father. You are truly the Son of God, *God from God, Light from Light, true God from true God.*[12] You are the beloved Son of the Father, the One in whom He is well pleased. I love You and adore You. *Venite adoremus!*

But – and here is a wonderful revelation that fills us with joy – this fullness of Divine life which is in Jesus Christ is meant to overflow from Him to us, to humankind in its entirety.

The divine Sonship which is in Christ by nature, and makes Him God's own and only Son, 'the only-begotten Son, who is in the bosom of the Father',[13] is meant to extend as far as us by grace, in such a way that Christ, in the Divine thought 'might be the first-born amongst many brethren'.[14]

We are here at the central point of the Divine plan: *the Divine adoption. It is from Jesus Christ, it is through Jesus Christ, that we receive it.* It was to confer adoption on us, says St Paul, that God sent His Son: 'God sent his Son born of a woman ... to enable us to be adopted as sons.'[15] The grace of Christ, Son of God, has been communicated to us to become in us the principle of adoption; it is on the fullness of Divine life and grace of Christ Jesus that we all have to draw ...

It is through Christ that we enter the family of God; it is from Him and through Him that grace comes to us, and consequently Divine life: 'I am the life';[16] 'I am come, that they may have life, and may have it more abundantly.'[17]

(Christ, the Life of the Soul, Part I, I.v)

---

1 Offertory of the Mass
2 Eph. 3:9
3 Eph. 1:21
4 1:3–10
5 John 1:14
6 Antiphon of the office of the Circumcision
7 John 5:26
8 Psalm 2:7; Hebr. 5:5
9 Col. 2:3
10 Col. 2:9
11 John 1:14
12 Nicene Creed
13 John 1:18
14 Rom. 8:29
15 Gal. 4:4–5 (Jerusalem)
16 John 11:25; 14:6
17 John 10:10

6. TO ONE OF HER SISTERS

Written for a postulant, Sœur Marie-Joseph de Notre Dame de Grâce, in July 1906.

Elizabeth had been made 'angel' to Sœur Marie-Joseph (that is, a fellow-sister teaching her the customs of the community), and she plays on that term in this poem, weaving it in with her main theme, *grace*: both sanctifying grace – supernatural life, as in the succeeding first extract from Marmion – and actual grace, prompting and guiding our actions.

How very rich you are –
        dear Sister, do you know?
And have you ever plumbed
        the mighty depth and height? –
A constancy of Love
        (I've come to you to show)
Hovers about your soul
        through every day and night.
Oh, simply look and see
        the Mystery! and how
It works within your heart
        (faith also has its eyes) –
The Holy Spirit's choice,
        His temple are you now:
You are no longer yours,
        and there your greatness lies.
Beneath the touch divine
        in silence live, that He
Imprint Himself in you –
        your Saviour's image know,
The likeness pre-ordained
        to be your destiny,

Mysterious! and yet . . .
>> our Maker writ it so.
For you become Himself:
>> truly, no longer you.
The transformation . . . yes,
>> each moment it occurs.
Give thanks, then, to the Lord
>> that this He wills to do –
Ah, may your being, deep,
>> make adoration hers.
Always believe in love!
>> Whatever be the case . . .
God in your heart's asleep,
>> you think? Well, understand
You're not to wake Him up!
>> for that's another grace –
That, little sister, then
>> He still has you in hand.
An *angel* sent to you,
>> I have to come and sing
Before I fly away
>> to rest in light above:
And . . . overflowing grace
>> to you I'll know to bring
When I shall live up there,
>> the Hearth and Home of love.
I'll guide you, ev'ry step
>> upon the road ahead,
In spreading over you
>> those angel-wings of mine,

That nevermore your feet
        may waver as you tread
That then, in everything
        you act by what's Divine.
And, tell me, isn't this
        that thing of precious worth –
Upon a solemn day
        the mission I was giv'n?
Ah! I'll be true to that,
        and even on the earth
I'd like to show'r on you
        all of the Gifts of heav'n.
Your *beauty* – that is what
        I'm jealous for! That you
Who bear the title 'spouse'
        will measure up to this,
Dear sister, always (that
        I dream that you may do)
Look to the Saviour's Cross
        where all your glory is.
Beneath the hand, be calm
        when it shall immolate,
As did your loved one, Christ.
        In ev'ry sorrow He
Stayed as a man of Strength –
        of sovereign peace His state
Up to the last heart's-woe
        – anguish – on Calvary.
Look at and imitate
        this Archetype divine,

Yes, be — whatever comes —
            a copy, really true:
You'll give the Father then
            huge glory, it will shine.
And, you His loving choice,
            He will look after you.

Notes

P 106

29 July 1906

'His temple are you now.'

'What is your motto?'
'God in me, I in Him.'
(Question put to Elizabeth, a week after her entry into Carmel, and her reply).

'Oh, my dear [Framboise], how happy one is when lives in intimacy with the good God, when one makes one's life a heart-to-heart, an exchange of love, when one knows how to find the Master in the depth of one's soul. Then one is never alone any more, and one has need of solitude so as to enjoy the presence of this adored Guest.' (Elizabeth, letter to Françoise de Sourdon, 28 April 1903).

> 'All-silent, let us gaze upon the sight
> To fix on Changeless Beauty with our eyes.'
> (Elizabeth, Poem 7)

BLESSED COLUMBA MARMION: The Portion of the Faithful Soul, through Grace.

Let us at this stage pause a moment to consider the greatness of the gift He makes to us. We shall have some idea of it if we look at what happens in the natural order.

Take minerals: they do not live; they do not contain any inner principle that might be the source of activity; minerals possess a participation in being, with certain properties, but their mode of being is very inferior. Take plants: they live, they move themselves harmoniously, in an unvarying way and following fixed laws, towards the perfection of their being; but this life is of the lowest grade, for plants lack consciousness. Though superior to that of plants, the life of animals is nevertheless limited to having senses and to the necessities of instinct. With man, we rise to a higher sphere: reason and free will characterize the life peculiar to a human being; but man is also matter. Above man are the angels, pure spirits whose life marks the highest degree of all in the domain of creation. Infinitely surpassing all these created lives, received by way of participation, there is the Divine life, life uncreated, life absolutely transcendent, fully autonomous and independent, above the strength of every creature; life necessary, subsistent in itself ... In this Divine life, which spreads out in all fullness, are to be found the source of all perfection and the principle of all bliss.

It is this life that God wants to communicate to us; participation in this life constitutes our holiness. And as, for us, there are degrees of this participation, the more the participation is extended, the higher is our holiness.

And let us not forget that it is solely through love that God has resolved to give Himself in this way ... As this love is Divine, the gift He gives is Divine also. God loves Divinely; He gives Himself. We are called to receive, in ineffable measure, this Divine communication; God means to give Himself to us, not only as Supreme Beauty, the object of contemplation, but to unite Himself to us, so as to make Himself, so far as is possible, but one with us ...

How does God effect this magnificent design by which He wishes to make us part of this life which exceeds the dimensions of our nature, which surpasses nature's rights and own energies, which is not called for by any of nature's demands, but which, without destroying that nature, showers on it a bliss undreamt-of by the human heart? How will God make us have ineffable 'fellowship with'[1] His divine life so as to make us sharers of His eternal beatitude?

By adopting us as His children ...

Now, we who are ... by nature, further from God than animals are from man, who are infinitely distant from God ... how can we be adopted by God?

It is here we find the marvel of the Divine wisdom, power and goodness. God gives us a mysterious sharing of His nature that we call 'grace': 'that ... you may be made partakers of the Divine nature'.[2]

Grace is an *interior quality*, produced in us by God, inhering in the soul, adorning the soul and making it pleasing to God ...

Grace, in a way whose depths elude us, makes us sharers of the nature of God: by grace, we are raised above our nature, we become, in a way, gods. We do not become equal to, but like God ...

For us, then, a sharing in this Divine life is effected by grace, in virtue of which our soul becomes capable of knowing God as God knows Himself; of loving God as He loves Himself; of rejoicing in God as God is filled with His own beatitude, and thus of living the life of God Himself ...

In relation to us, the life to which God raises us is supernatural, that is to say, exceeding the dimensions, the strength, the rights and the exigencies of our nature ...

Upon our natural life is grafted, so to speak, another life of which grace is the principle; grace becomes in us the source of actions and of operations which are super-natural and tend towards a divine end: possessing God one day, and rejoicing in Him ...

(*Christ, the Life of the Soul*, Part I, I.iii–iv)

I have told you that holiness for us is nothing other than the complete flowering, the full development, of that first grace which is our divine adoption, grace given at baptism ... and by which we become children of God and brothers of Christ Jesus. The very substance of holiness is to draw from this initial grace of adoption, to make them bear fruit, all those treasures and riches it contains and that God causes to flow from it. Christ ... is the model of our divine filiation; moreover, He has merited that it should be given to us, and He has Himself established the means by which it comes to us.

But, Jesus having made that grace possible for us, the bringing of it into being within us is the work of the Blessed Trinity. However, and not without grounds, that work is attributed[3] specially to the Holy Spirit. Why is that? Always for the same reason. This grace of adoption is purely gratuitous and has its source in love:[4] now, in the adorable Trinity the Holy Spirit is substantial Love ...

And from the moment of the infusion of grace in us by baptism, the Holy Spirit dwells in us with the Father and the Son: 'If any one love me', says Our Lord, '... my Father will love him, and we will come to him, and will make our ABODE with him' (John 14:23). Grace makes our soul the temple of the Holy Trinity; our soul, adorned by grace, is truly the abode of God; He dwells in us, not only as He does in all things, by His essence and His power whereby He sustains and preserves every created being in existence, but in a way altogether particular and intimate, as the object of super-natural knowledge and love. And because grace thus unites us to God, and is the reason for and measure of our charity, it is above all the Holy Spirit who is said to 'dwell in us', not as though it were in a manner personal to Him to the exclusion of the Father and the Son, but because He proceeds from love and it is He who unites the Father and the Son: He 'shall abide with you, and shall be in you', said Our Lord.[5]

(*Ibid.*, Part I, VI.iv)

When we possess Divine grace within us, we fulfil the wishing of Our Lord: we 'dwell in Him' and He 'dwells in us'; He dwells in us with the Father and the Holy Spirit (John 14:23). The Holy Trinity, truly living in us as in a temple, does not remain inactive there, but dwells in us to sustain us constantly in order that our soul can exercise its super-natural activity: 'My Father has never ceased working, and I too must be at work.'[6]

(*Ibid.*, Part II, V.ii)

By this [by staying united to Christ, Head of His Mystical Body and beloved Son of the Father] we shall tend towards the perfection of our Model by uninterrupted growth, for Christ dwells in us, with His Father, by Whom we are loved (John 14:23), with the Holy Spirit Who guides us by His inspiration: that is the source of an incessant and fruitful progress towards heaven . . .

(*Ibid.*, Part II, VI.viii)

[1]   1 John 1:3
[2]   2 Pet. 1:4
[3]   See 1 John 3:1
[4]   John 14:17
[5]   See note 54 in the Notes to Translator's Introduction.
[6]   John 5:17 (Knox)

Elizabeth (left), at the age of ten, with her mother and sister, Guite.

7. THE HEART WOUNDED BY INFINITY

Elizabeth wrote this poem in 1902 for Sœur Agnès de Jésus-Maria.

Do you not hear the silence sing on high?
Already, Sister! hear the hymn of love.
Suffering? exile? – both of them gone by:
Forgotten, as we greet Day-break above.
Eternal Splendour shining! Don't you see
The Trinity bend over us? and, clear
The heavens open . . .! Now, the call – it's He!
Let us then gather, for the Bridegroom's here.

Do you not see the cloud that's full of light –
It reaches *us*, this blaze from splendent skies! –
All-silent, let us gaze upon the sight
To fix on Changeless Beauty with our eyes.
A look from Christ . . . as water is made clear,
God's purity is formed in us by this.
That He may deify, let us dwell here –
Our souls in His soul, and our eyes in His.

Himself, He comes to kiss us! so to be
Our love beyond the telling. In His shade
(He hovers over, to protect us) we
By sight of Him are fruitful virgins made.
The Father's Splendour, beautiful; how bright
Is Christ our Lord. Lit by Divinity,
He is himself a burning hearth of Light
That wraps His own about with radiancy.

Then, let us love; all else can disappear.
Identify with God — how so? By love!
Let's wait not till His glory shines; we here
Can gaze on Him as do the blest above.
He's ours, and He belongs to us, by grace.
We — as in Heav'n — adore Him now, the same.
But very soon we'll gaze upon His Face
And on our brows will shine His Holy Name.

When will it end at last, our waiting-state?
When, offer up ourselves as though to fire?
Let us adore our dear Lamb as we wait.
To purify us — this is His desire.
Do you not feel a passion now to show
To Christ a little of *His* love? That way
I want to die: to say 'I love You, so
As You did, I yield up myself today!'

Teresa must be smiling up in Heav'n —
Another who'd run off, to go above!
God hadn't that in view . . . what was she giv'n?
A Victim-Martyr, she who died of Love.
For virgins' martyrdom will never fade
Whose hearts *Infinity has wounded thus.*
A holy torment, Love itself the blade.
Then, Barb of Fire, pierce also now through us!

Teresa: i.e. of Avila (*Life*, Ch.I)

> 'Eternal splendour shining! Don't you see
> The Trinity bend over us?'

'On the evening of Palm Sunday I had a strong attack [of her illness] and I thought the hour had at last arrived when I was going to fly off into the infinite regions to gaze on that Trinity unveiled which was already my dwelling-place here below . . .' (Elizabeth, June 1906, to Germaine de Gemeaux).

BLESSED COLUMBA MARMION: Participation in the Bliss of the Trinity through the Incarnation and our Redemption.

(What the Incarnation and the Sacrifice on the Cross made possible for us): God desires, with an infinite will, that we should be holy; He wishes it because He is holy Himself;[1] because He has placed in that sanctification the glory He expects from us,[2] and the joy with which He desires to satisfy us.[3]

But what is 'being holy'? We are creatures, our holiness only exists through participation in the holiness of God; we should therefore, so as to understand it, go up all the way to God. He alone is holy by essence, or rather, He is holiness itself . . .

Human reason can arrive at establishing the existence of this holiness of the supreme Being, holiness which is an attribute, a perfection of the Divine nature considered in itself.

But Revelation has brought us a new light.

Here we should lift up the eyes of our soul with reverence, all the way to the sanctuary of the Adorable Trinity;

we should listen to what Christ Jesus – as much to nourish our piety as to exercise our faith – has willed either to reveal to us Himself or to propound to us through His Church, about the inner life of God.

In God, as you know, there are three distinct Persons, the Father, the Son and the Holy Spirit, yet all three having but one and the same unique nature or Divine essence. Infinite intelligence, the Father has perfect knowledge of His perfections, He expresses this knowledge in one unique Utterance: it is the Word,[4] the living and substantial utterance, the adequate expression, of who the Father is. In uttering this Word, the Father begets His Son, to whom He communicates all His essence, His nature, His perfections, His life ... The Son equally belongs entirely to His Father, is entirely given up to Him by a total donation which pertains to His nature as Son. And from this mutual donation of only one and the same love proceeds, as from one unique principle, the Holy Spirit who seals the union of the Father and the Son, in being their substantial and living love.

This mutual communication of the three Persons, this adherence, infinite and full of love, of the Divine Persons between themselves, assuredly constitutes a new revelation of holiness in God: this is the union of God with Himself in the unity of His nature and the Trinity of the Persons.

God finds all His essential beatitude in this inexpressibly one and fruitful life: to exist, God has need only of Himself and His perfections. Finding all bliss in the perfections of His nature and in the ineffable society of His Persons, He has no need of any creature; it is to Himself, in Himself, in His Trinity, that He relates the glory welling forth from His infinite perfections.

As you know, God has decreed that we be allowed to enter into a sharing of this inner life, proper to Him alone; He wishes to communicate this fathomless beatitude that has its source in the fullness of the infinite Being.

That being so – and this is the first point in St Paul's

exposition of the Divine plan – our holiness will be *to adhere to God, God known and loved*, no longer simply as the Author of creation but *as He knows and loves Himself* in the bliss of the Trinity; this is to be united to God to the extent of sharing His inner life . . .

(*Christ, the Life of the Soul*, Part I, I.ii–iii)

---

1   Levit. 11:44; 1 Pet. 1:16
2   John 15:8
3   John 16:22
4   'In the beginning was the Word, and the Word was with God, and the Word was God': John 1:1

Elizabeth in the summer of 1898, at or nearly eighteen.

8. THE HEAVEN OF GLORY AND THE HEAVEN OF FAITH

Another poem which Elizabeth wrote for the patronal feast-day of Mère Germaine, this one in 1902.

At Elizabeth's beatification process, Sœur Agnès referred to this poem in saying 'When we used to go, at recreation, to work in the garden, we would sing together (and with what heart!)'.

Voice of Heaven
We who are bathed in Light, within the 'Three' –
The Face of God, the splendour of its rays –
See, by those shinings, into Mystery:
They ever show new secrets, Heaven's days.

Infinite Being! Depth unsoundable!
Delighted, *lost* in Your Divinity –
O Trinity, God thrice-immutable,
We see Yourself in Your own clarity.

Voice of Earth
The saints in Heav'n . . . but, also, here below
Souls come and merge themselves in such a Love,
In mystery and night this happens so –
God satisfies: in dark, in Day above.

Through everything . . . on earth: already we're
Possessing You, our Peace and vision! (for,
As in one light we gather, there and here,
We lose ourselves in God, for evermore!

Voice of Heaven
As sharers, *now*, in God's own Essence, you
Possess all we possess in Heaven . . . See! —
You have not yet the joy we have, that's true:
But as for giving — you give more than we.

And when one loves, how good it is to give!
(You *can* be giving, every hour and place.)
Oh, give God glory while on earth you live —
By self-oblation. Seize on this high grace!

Second stanza, line 2: Another version has: 'We are in communion with (*communions à*) Your Divinity.'

Notes

P 80

15 June 1902

'As sharers, *now*, in God's own Essence . . .'

'"When shall I go to see the face of God?"[1] And yet, "as the sparrow has found herself a house", as "the turtle a nest for herself, where she may lay her young ones",[2] so Laudem Gloriae – while waiting to be transferred to the Holy Jerusalem, *"beata pacis visio"* – has found her retreat, her beatitude, her anticipated Heaven where she begins her life of eternity.' (Elizabeth, *Last Retreat*, Sixteenth Day)

'Fortunately, we can dwell in Him even in our time of exile [on earth].' (Elizabeth, letter to Canon Angles, 9 May 1906)

BLESSED COLUMBA MARMION: In Heaven, sight; on earth, faith.

Let us not think it may be a presumption on our part to want to turn into reality an ideal so sublime. No, this very desire is God's own; it is His eternal thinking with regard to us: He predestined us to be made conformable to the image of His Son.[3] The more we are conformed to His Son, the more the Father loves us because the more we are united to Him. When He sees a soul fully transformed into His Son, He surrounds that soul with His altogether special protection, with the tenderest of His providential care; He showers on it His blessings, He places no bounds on the communication of His graces: there is the secret of the largesses of God.

Oh, let us thank our Father in heaven for having given us His Son, Christ Jesus as our model, so that we have but to look at Him to know what we have to do: '*Hear Him.*'[4]

Christ has said to us: 'I have given you an example, that as I have done to you, so you do also.'[5] He has left us His example, so that we might walk in His footsteps.[6] He is the only way we must follow: 'I am the way'.[7] One who follows that way does not walk in darkness but comes to the light of life.[8] There is the model that faith reveals to us, a model transcendent and yet accessible: 'Look, and make it according to the pattern'.[9]

The soul of Our Lord, at every moment, contemplated the Divine essence: in that same gaze, His soul saw the ideal conceived by God for humanity, and each one of His actions was the expression of that ideal. Let us, then, lift up our eyes, let us love to know Christ Jesus more and more, to study His life in the Gospels, to follow His mysteries in the admirable order established by the Church herself in her liturgical cycle, from Advent to Pentecost; let us open the eyes of our faith, and live in such a way as to reproduce in us the features of this exemplar, to conform our existence to His words and His acts. This model is Divine and visible; He shows us God acting in the midst of us and sanctifying, in His humanity, all our actions, even the most ordinary; all our feelings, even the most intimate; all our sufferings, even those most deep.

Let us contemplate Him, this model, but with faith. We are sometimes tempted to envy the contemporaries of Jesus who were able to see Him, to follow Him, to listen to Him. But faith makes Him present to us also, in a presence not less efficacious for our souls. Christ has said it to us Himself: 'BLESSED are they that have not seen, and have believed'.[10] This is to make us understand that it is not less advantageous for us to remain in contact with Jesus by faith than to have seen Him in the flesh. He whom we see living and acting when we read the Gospels, or when we celebrate His mysteries, is God's own Son. We have said everything when we have said of Christ: 'You are the Son of the living God',[11] and there we have the fundamental aspect of the Divine Model of our souls.

Let us contemplate Him, not with a contemplation that is abstract, exterior, theoretical, cold, but with a contemplation full of love, attentive to seize upon the smallest features of this model to reproduce them in our own existence, but above all that basic and primordial disposition of Christ, of living for His Father. All of His life can be said to come down to that feature; all the virtues of Christ are the effect of this orientation of His soul towards the Father; and this orientation is itself but the product of that ineffable union by which, in Jesus, the whole of humanity is drawn into that Divine impetus which carries the Son towards His Father.

(*Christ, the Life of the Soul*, Part I, II.iv)

1 Psalm 42:2, Jerusalem (Douai, 41:3)
2 Psalm 83:4 (Jerusalem, 84:3)
3 Rom. 8:29
4 Matt. 17:5; Mark 9:6
5 John 13:15
6 1 Pet. 2:21
7 John 14:6
8 John 8:12
9 Exod. 25:40
10 John 20:29
11 Matt. 16:16

Elizabeth, twenty-two, in the month before her Profession.

9. WHO IS LIKE TO GOD?

Elizabeth wrote this poem in 1906, for the sixteenth anniversary of the taking of the habit by Sœur Louise de Gonzague. It is dated 29 September, the Feast of St Michael the Archangel. His name, Michael, means 'Who is like God?' – the ringing answer to Lucifer's 'I will not serve'.

In fêting you today,
> your anniversary,
I see you from this hill
> that our Redeemer trod.
Today our hearts are joined
> to sing, in harmony
That challenge Michael made:
> *Who, then, is like to God?*

Who, then, is like to God? –
> a splendid motto there
For one who is afire
> to bring the self to naught,
Distilling-pure one's life
> to aid the Church; in prayer
Within a silence deep,
> a recollection sought.

Who, then, is like to God? . . .
> that truth we shall discern
If we but – there to stay –
> swift to the Cross will go.

For He whom it supports
         will teach us, and we'll learn
The rights His love has won –
         what love to Him we owe.

Who, then, is like to God? . . .
         To see the Master here
Annihilate His self
         before His Father thus,
Means now that, in our turn,
         we want to disappear . . .
So we'll resemble Him,
         abasement, too, from us!

Who, then, is like to God? . . .
         To be empow'red to give
Our homage to his Power
         as to his Majesty,
We ought, for witness true
         each moment that we live,
To prize the lovely thing
         that is Humility.

Let's cultivate with care
         the gentle violet, then –
How pleasing to our Spouse,
         O perfumed one, are you!

So happy will He be
        to pick that flower when,
With evening, comes at last
        the heav'nly Rendezvous.

Down that *two-fold abyss*
        ourselves now let us throw –
Immensity of God,
        the nothingness of us! –
Our worship of Him then
        can rise up higher, so
We'll praise our mighty Lord
        (His Name be glorious).

He likes to find a soul
        with such an attitude,
A self-negated soul,
        one with humility:
He rushes to her then
        in all His plentitude –
Into His inmost heart
        admits her rapidly.

Another version has, for the last line: 'To consummate the divine union'.

Corridor in the Dijon Carmel.

Notes

P 118

29 September 1906

> 'Immensity of God,
> the nothingness of us!'

Preliminary thought: Consider why the word 'self-important' has bad vibes, the word 'self-effacing' good ones.

G. K. Chesterton: 'If I had only one sermon to preach, it would be a sermon against Pride . . . let us suppose any place where men of motley but ordinary types assemble . . . an average handful of human beings. Let us suppose that the enquirer, politely approaching this group, opens the conversation in a chatty way by saying "Theologians are of opinion that it was one of the superior angelic intelligences seeking to become the supreme object of worship, instead of finding his natural joy in worshipping, which dislocated the providential design and frustrated the full joy and completion of the cosmos" . . . we may well admit that such a company will find it something of a strain to accept the formula in the above form . . . Even if he states the matter in the simplified form, that Pride is the worst of the Seven Deadly Sins, he will only produce a vague and rather unfavourable impression that he is preaching. But he is only preaching what everybody else is practising; or at least is wanting everybody else to practise.

'Let the scientific enquirer continue to cultivate the patience of science. Let him linger . . . in the place of popular entertainment whatever it may be, and take very careful note (if necessary in a note-book) of the way in which ordinary human beings do really talk about each other . . . if he will listen carefully, he will observe a certain tone taken towards friends, foes and acquaintances; a tone which is, on the whole, creditably genial and considerate, though not without strong likes and dislikes. He will hear abundant if sometimes bewildering allusion to the well-known weaknesses of Old George; but many excuses also, and a certain generous pride in conceding that Old George is quite the gentleman when drunk or that he told the policeman off proper. Some celebrated idiot, who is always spotting winners that never win, will be treated with almost tender derision; and, especially among the poorest, there will be a true Christian pathos in the reference to those who have been "in trouble" for habits like burglary and petty larceny. And as all these queer types are called up like ghosts by the incantation of gossip, the enquirer will gradually form the impression that there is one kind of man, probably only one kind of man, perhaps, only one man, who is really disliked. The voices take on quite a different tone in speaking of him; there is a hardening and solidification of disapproval and a new coldness in the air. And this will be all the more curious because, by the current modern theories of social or anti-social action, it will not be at all easy to say why he should be such a monster; or what exactly is the matter with him. It will hinted at only in singular figures of speech, about a gentleman who is mistakenly convinced that he owns the street; or sometimes that he owns the earth. Then one of the social critics will say, "'E comes in 'ere and 'e thinks 'e's Gawd Almighty." Then the scientific enquirer will shut his note-book with a snap and retire from the scene, possibly after paying for any drinks he may have consumed in the cause of social science. He has got what he wanted. He has been intellectually justified. The man in the pub has precisely repeated, word for word, the theological formula about Satan.' (Essay, *If I had only One Sermon to Preach*).

'Difficulties can easily be raised, of course . . . by the accident of words being used in different senses. For instance, when we speak of somebody being "proud of" something, as of a man being proud of his wife or a people proud of its heroes, we really mean something that is the very opposite of pride. For it implies that the man thinks that something outside himself is needed to give him great glory . . .' (*ibid.*)

109

BLESSED COLUMBA MARMION: 'Humility is walking in the Truth' (St Teresa of Avila)

[*Marmion speaks of what one may call the 'is-ness' of the situation. That 'is-ness' means that humility accords with simple reality; pride denies reality.*]

Scripture, you know, has some strange expressions for signifying, in human language, the situation the prideful are placed in before the face of God. What does it say? That God '*resisteth the proud*'.[1] If it is a terrible thing for a created being to be abandoned by God, what is it when God sets himself to resist him? . . .

What then is there that is so bad, so contrary to God, in pridefulness, for God to push it far away from Him, with such force?

The reason for this antagonism is drawn from the very nature of the Divine holiness. God is the beginning and the end, the alpha and the omega,[2] of all things; He is the first cause of every created being and the source of every perfection. All existence comes from Him, all good derives from Him; but, also every creature has to return to Him, every glory has to be referred to Him. God has made everything for His glory: 'The Lord hath made all things for Himself'.[3] In us, such conduct would be egoism, supreme disorderdness; in God, to Whom the term egoism can in no way have application, it is a necessity based on His very nature. It is of the essence of the holiness of God to relate everything to His own glory; otherwise God would not be God, because He would be subordinated to another end than Himself . . .

Now, what does the prideful man do? He tries to steal from God, in order to appropriate to himself this glory that God alone merits and of which He is so jealous. The prideful man lifts himself up, makes himself the centre; he glorifies his own self, in his person, in his perfection, in his works; it is only in himself that he sees the principle of all that he has and of all that he is: he considers he owes nothing to anybody, not even to God; he wants, for his own profit, to deprive God of this Divine attribute of being First Principle and Last End. Doubtless, in theory, he may think that everything comes from God; but in practice he acts and lives as if everything came from himself ...

Our Divine Saviour, so merciful and so compassionate, renews the same lessons for us under the colours – such strong colours and so impressive – of the parable of the Pharisee and the Publican. Look at the Pharisee: this is a man convinced of his importance; full of, and sure of, himself: the 'I' of this man flaunts itself in his words, in his attitude. He stands upright in the careless posture of someone who is aware of his personal worth and his personal perfection, who owes nothing to anybody, and who, conversely, reckons he has no need of anything. He complacently parades before God all that he does. It is true that he gives thanks to Him; but, remarks St Bernard, this false homage is merely a lie added to the pride; the pharisee has 'a double heart',[4] as the Psalmist puts it; the contempt he has for the publican shows that he believes himself to be much more perfect than him, and so it is to himself that he really reserves the glory which in appearance he gives to God. He asks nothing from God, because he considers he has need of nothing, he is sufficient unto himself; instead, he exhibits his conduct for the approbation of God. Can one not hear him saying: 'My God, you must be very pleased with me, for I am truly irreproachable; I am not like other men, not like this publican.' At heart, this personage is, practically speaking, convinced that all his perfection comes from himself ...

As for the other actor in the scene, the publican, what does he do? He stands at a distance, not daring even to raise his eyes, for he feels himself to be a wretch. Does he think he has any claims by which he might be able to prevail before God? None. He is aware of bringing nothing but his sins: 'My God, I am nothing but an offender, have pity on me.' He relies only on the Divine Mercy; he looks for nothing, he hopes for nothing, except from that. All his confidence, all his hope, he places in God.

Now, how does God act with these two men? Very differently. 'I say unto you', declares Christ Jesus, that the publican 'went down to his house justified, rather than the other', the pharisee.[5] Yet, this publican – was he not a sinner? Assuredly. The pharisee, on the other hand – was he not, at least exteriorly, a faithful observer of the law of Moses? No less certainly, yes. But *he*, full of himself, showed by his contempt for the publican that in his own heart he raised himself up because of good actions carried out; he wanted to take God's place. And God repulses him: 'He hath scattered the proud in the conceit of their heart'.[6] To the poor publican who humbles himself He gives on the contrary His grace in abundance: 'God ... giveth grace to the humble'.[7]

And Christ Jesus, in concluding the parable, Himself lays down the fundamental law which governs our relations with God; He brings out the essential lesson that we ought to learn from it: 'Every one that exalteth himself, shall be humbled; and he that humbleth himself, shall be exalted.'[8]

You see to what extent pride is enemy to the union of the soul with God; there is in us, says St Thomas, no sin, no tendency, which more bears the character of an obstacle to the Divine communications. And as God is the principle of every grace, pride is for the soul the most terrible of all dangers; whereas there is no surer way of attaining sanctity and of finding God than humility. It is pride which, above all, stands in the way of God giving Himself; if there were no more pride in souls, God would give Himself to them fully. Humility, indeed, is a virtue so fundamental that without it, says the Abbot of Clairvaux, all the other virtues crumble away ...

Humility is the practical and continuous avowal of our wretchedness, and this avowal attracts the eyes of God. The rags and the wounds of the poor are their pleadings; do they seek in fact to hide them? Very much the opposite; they display them, in order to touch people's hearts. In the same way, we ought not to seek to dazzle God by our perfection, but rather to attract His pity by the avowal of our weakness . . .

When we recognize, indeed, that of ourselves we are weak, poor, wretched, infirm, we implicitly proclaim the power, the wisdom, the holiness, the goodness of God; doing that is to render homage to the Divine plenitude, and such homage is so pleasing to God that He bends down to the humble soul to fill it with good things. As St Bernard, again, says: 'Our heart is a vessel destined to receive grace: for it to be able to contain it in abundance, it must be empty of self-love and vain glory. When humility has there prepared a vast capacity to be filled, grace floods in upon it, for there is a close affinity between grace and humility.' Nothing, then, is more efficacious than this virtue for meriting grace, for retaining it within us, or recovering it if we have lost it.

There exists yet another reason for the liberality of God in regard to humble souls: God knows that the humble soul will not take pleasure in the graces He gives it so as to draw forth glory from them; God sees that this soul will not appropriate to itself the Divine gifts, as the proud do, but will refer back to heaven all glory and all praise; and this is why, if one is permitted to put in thus, God has no fear of letting the abundance of His favours flow in on it: the soul will not abuse this, it will not turn off course the Divine intentions.

The more we want to approach God, then, the more we ought to anchor ourselves deeply in humility.

(*Christ, the Life of the Monk*, XI.i)

Let us, then, ask Him [the Holy Spirit] to enter into us; there to live, there to increase the abundance of His gifts. Fervent prayer is one condition of His entering our souls.

Humility is another. Let us present ourselves to Him with the personal conviction of our inner poverty; that disposition of soul is excellent for receiving Him of whom the Church sings: *Sine tuo numine, nihil est in homine, nihil est innoxium*:[9] 'Without Your divine empowering, there is nothing in man, nothing but that which is harmful to him' . . .

(*Christ in His Mysteries*, XVII.v)

(These are) the sentiments which ought to animate us in our quest for holiness: a deep humility because of our weakness, an absolute confidence in Christ Jesus. Our supernatural life swings between two poles: on the one hand we ought to have a personal conviction of our powerlessness to attain to perfection without the aid of God; on the other hand we ought to be filled with an unshakeable hope of finding everything in the grace of Christ Jesus.

(ibid., XX.iv)

For – and I here come to an important point – humility is truth. Some minds think that, to be humble, one has to deny one's natural gifts or the graces that God gives us. 'There are', says St Teresa [of Avila], on this subject, 'people who think they are making an act of humility in refusing to recognize the gifts the Lord bestows on them.' Is one there honouring God? Nothing is more misplaced. 'Let us understand well', adds the Saint – yes, let us understand it well; it is nothing but the exact truth: 'God bestows on us [these gifts] without our having in any way merited them.' What, then, should one do in the presence of Divine graces? Recognize that God alone is the author and the principle of them: 'every perfect gift is from above, coming down from the Father of lights',[10] and render thanksgiving to Him. 'But if a present we have been given remains unknown to us, how will it make love arise in our hearts? It is beyond doubt that the more we see ourselves rich, whereas our personal indigence is well known to us, the more also we advance in virtue and in true humility ...'[11]

(Christ, the Ideal of the Monk, XI.vii)

[1] 1 Pet. 5:5; James 4:6.
[2] Apoc. 22:13.
[3] Prov. 16:4.
[4] Psalm 11:3 (Jerusalem, 12:2).
[5] Luke 18:14.
[6] Luke 1:51.
[7] James 4:6; 1 Pet. 5:5.
[8] Luke 18:14.
[9] Sequence, *Veni Sancte Spiritus.*
[10] James 1:17.
[11] St Teresa, *Life,* Ch. 10.

Marmion, a seminarian at Clonliffe in 1876, aged about nineteen.

10. CHRISTMAS 1904

A remarkable expression of Elizabeth's thought. The Christ Child comes to earth as a Lover, a Suitor.

> Just a humble stable it is . . .
> With the *Word of God* cradled there!
> Adorable mystery, this,
> That angels reveal, everywhere . . .
> *Gloria in excelsis Deo!*

To pour our floods of love for us – this brought
(Compelled Him!) the Almighty from above:
A heart to *understand* this He has sought;
To fix in it the dwelling of His love.
In Heaven's depths – the gap from Him forgot –
He dreamt that we'd be joined with Him, and thus . . . .
Ah, see Him come here, like an arrow-shot!
To consummate that fusion here with us.

> Oh, mystery; oh, depths no-one can scan –
> That Uncreated Being turns to me!
> At ev'ry moment – on earth, yet – I can
> Look on Him clear! in Faith's own clarity.

As to my holy Patron, Jesus said,
Lovingly: 'Do you want to live with Me?
'Elizabeth (my grace about you spread),
'*One* with you – this is what I wish to be!
'To take you for my bride, I come today;
'To immolate you, be consoled by you.
'Be jealous of My honour always. Say
'You'll seek to give Me joy by all you do.'

Oh, mystery; oh, depths no-one can scan:
Consider! the Eternal bending near
To me! Whatever comes, by faith I can
Touch, and unite myself with Him, and here.

'Look at Me! you will better comprehend
'Annihilation, gift of you to Me
'(Exalting Me, you always must descend –
'Abasement let your peace and comfort be!).
'It's there, and always, that the meeting is.
'To little ones I show Myself. I teach:
'Annihilate your self, to find by this
'The hidden God your being longs to reach.'

Oh, mystery; oh, depths no-one can scan –
This Being, Infinite, wrapped up in me!
Whatever comes – by faith, on earth – I can
Be lost in Him! enfold Him, utterly!

You seek that I (O Master and Adored)
Be like an altar-host. In charity
You want to live on earth for ever, Lord,
Incarnate, here among humanity!
Your dream: that, mounting to the Father, would
Rise Sacrifice and Adoration. Thus
You'll cover by effusion of Your blood
The earth, and in this way be saving us.

Oh, mystery unsoundable! That now
My heart Your humble sacrament's become!
Oh glorify, in Him, the Father: bow
In silence and in recollection. Come!

Notes

P 91

Christmas 1904

> 'Oh, mystery; oh, depths no-one can scan –
> That Uncreated Being turns to me!'

'Arise, make haste, my love, my dove, my beautiful one, and come. For winter is now past, the rain is over and gone. The flowers have appeared in our land' (Song of Songs, 2:10–12)

The soul's response: '... a self-forgetting gift of self' (from description of the 'divine union in terms of marriage' of the soul and God: Conrad Pepler, OP, *The English Religious Heritage*)

BLESSED COLUMBA MARMION:
The Bridegroom's call, and the soul's response.

> The gift par excellence which God makes to the human creature is that of the grace of supernatural adoption in Jesus Christ, the Incarnate Word. The Sovereign Being, infinitely perfect, who neither depends on nor has need of anyone, lets His immeasurable Love overflow upon His creatures, to elevate them to the extent of a sharing of His Life and His Bliss ...
>
> We hear Christ Jesus Himself more than once compare the Kingdom of God to a nuptial banquet; God, in His Word and by His Word, calls souls to the feast of Divine union.
>
> (*Sponsa Verbi*, I)

But, you know, Christ does not separate Himself from His mystical body. Before ascending into heaven, Jesus bequeathed to His Church His riches and His mission ...

118

Endowed with the riches of Christ, the Church is introduced by Him into the palace of the King ...

(*Christ, the Ideal of the Monk*, XIII.ii)

If you abandon yourself without reserve to the Divine action of the Sacred Humanity of Jesus, He will carry you along with Him in that Divine current which ever flows like an impetuous torrent in the bosom of the Word. There your little personality will be lost and will disappear in deep adoration and perfect love ...

(Letter of Marmion, 21 September, 1910)[1]

You must throw yourself into His arms with your eyes shut. You must make an act of complete *abandon* to God; give yourself to Him, once and for all, without reserve ... I understand that such-or-such thing makes you suffer, but all that is accidental. What is essential is that you belong altogether to God. Consider yourself as God's 'thing' and never take yourself back ...

(Letter of Marmion, 1906)[1]

---

[1] Quoted in *Union with God according to the letters of Dom Marmion* by Dom Raymund Thibaut, OSB, London, 1935.

119

11. THE CARMELITE

One manuscript of this poem bears the inscription, in Latin: 'The one thing necessary' (stanza 3). It was written, in the first year of Elizabeth's novitiate, for St Martha's Day, feast of the non-choral Sisters, 29 July 1902.

She's one self-given, is a Carmelite —
A sacrifice, who's wholly occupied
To render God His glory (yet how bright
Her calvary! with Jesus, crucified).
Having her God, a Victim, in her gaze,
Light flashed within her soul, and that is why,
Knowing her soaring mission in its rays,
She cried, her wounded heart cried, 'Here am I!'

A Carmelite is one invaded: how?
Christ-filled, she's one who can, unceasingly,
Give Christ; for God made choice of her, and now
Like Mary, always at His feet she'll be.
Look well, then, at this captive who remains
In prayer that knows no interruption: for,
Soul caught and taken, she is now in chains —
Her Christ, and no distraction any more!

A Carmelite: a soul adoring! one
Surrendered to God's action, all, entire;
Whatever comes — in Large Communion,
Her heart uplifted, burning with God's fire!

'The one thing necessary' she has found:
God's Being, Light and Love. She'll intercede –
Her prayer a cloak that wraps the world around:
In that way – an apostle then indeed!

This, too: a soul that's closed, a Carmelite –
Closed up to things that happen here below;
Yet, also, wholly open and alight
To look on what the eye can never know.
And God, the Eagle, bears her in the air –
His light upon high summits like the sun –
To give her roof, the Father's dwelling there,
With God; consumed entirely; with Him one!

Notes

P 83

29 July 1902

> 'She's one self-given, is a Carmelite.'

'Did I ever tell you [what is to be] my name in Carmel? "Marie Elizabeth of the Trinity". It seems to me that that name indicates a particular vocation, isn't it beautiful? I so much love this mystery of the Holy Trinity, it is an abyss in which I lose myself!' (Elizabeth, letter to Canon Angles, 14 June 1901)

'O my beloved Christ, crucified by love, I would like to be a spouse of your Heart, I would like to cover You with glory, I would like to love You – even to dying of it!' (Elizabeth, Prayer to the Trinity)

'He *fascinates*, He carries one away; under His gaze the horizon becomes so beautiful, so vast, so luminous. You see, I love Him passionately, and in Him I have everything! It is through Him, beneath His radiance, that I must view all things, approach everything I do! . . . Look at Mary Magdalen – was she captivated! Since you need to live beyond yourself, live in Him; it is so simple.' (Elizabeth, letter to Françoise de Sourdon, 24 July 1902)

'I was nearly fourteen when one day, during my thanksgiving [after Holy Communion], I felt myself irresistibly urged to choose Him as my only Spouse, and without delay I bound myself to Him by a vow of virginity. We said nothing to each other, but we gave ourselves, one to the other, in being so strongly in love, that with me the resolution to be wholly His became more definite still. Another time, after Holy Communion, it seemed to me that the word "Carmel" was being pronounced in my soul, and I had no other thought than to bury self behind its grille.' (*Souvenirs*, account of Elizabeth's words)

BLESSED COLUMBA MARMION: Spouse of Christ.

Is not every baptised soul in some way the spouse of the Word? That is true. It was not only to the virgins, it was to all the faithful of the church of Corinth that St Paul wrote: 'I have espoused you to one husband, that I may present you as a chaste virgin to Christ.'[1] In baptism, indeed, the soul freely renounces[2] Satan, his pomps and his works, the world and its maxims, to adhere to Christ Jesus, to consecrate herself to His service. The grace of the Spirit of Love gives one over to God, renders one worthy of the favours of the celestial Spouse and gives one the right to claim the measureless joys of the eternal Kingdom that Our Lord himself has compared to those of a wedding-feast.

How holy and sanctifying already is this union of the baptised soul with Christ!

However, the union is much more close, the quality of spouse shines out with much more splendour, in the case of souls consecrated to Christ by the vows of religion ...

(Sponsa Verbi, I)

(Unreserved response): Fidelity, in all things and constant, necessarily leads the soul to 'live for the Word': *Verbo vivere* ...

For the soul, what in fact is 'to live'? The soul lives by the movement and the exercise of her faculties. She 'lives for the Word' when nothing within her either is in movement or starts into motion except for the interests and the glory of her Spouse; when she applies her memory, her imagination, her intelligence, her heart, her will, all her powers, all her activity to the service of the Word, to know Him, love Him, make Him known and make Him loved. The soul that lives for the Spouse does not seek in anything her own satisfaction, or her personal interest, but solely the good pleasure and glory of her Lord.

She is jealous in a holy way for the honour of her Spouse:

the cowardices, the infidelities, the injuries inflicted by so many souls, are wounds to herself, they stimulate her ardour and her generosity: 'A fainting hath taken hold of me, because of the wicked that forsake Thy law.'[3] She gives herself over entire, she gives over all that she has, all that she is, that the Spouse may be honoured, exalted, loved. Making her own the prayer of Jesus: 'Father, glorify Thy Son',[4] she employs herself, without let up, to effecting this glorifying of the Word; in herself first of all, in others afterwards. There, in a true sense, is to be seen devotedness, 'devotion', a generous, prompt, cheerful, ready movement of the generous soul; one which causes her, forgetful of herself, of her ease, of her tranquility, of her repose, of her desires, to preoccupy herself above all with the will of her Spouse, with His interests, with those of His Church.

Now, what, in this field, is the driving principle that sustains the soul, and stimulates her? What is the motive-power which uplifts her and transports her? It is love. Master of the will, love possesses all the avenues of her heart, all the powers of her soul, all the springs of her activity. Given up to love, the soul no longer has anything of her own, nor does she live any more for herself; she belongs wholly and entirely to her Beloved. 'What is "to love" if it is not to have, in everything and everywhere, the same will; to the extent of an entire extirpation of the least contrary desire and a total subjection of one's heart?'[5]

A love of that kind is transforming; it causes the soul to be like its Spouse. Listen to St Bernard (from whom we have borrowed the theme of our discussion) sing of the astonishing grandeur of this union: 'Such a conformity with the divine will *marries* the soul with the Word, to Whom she is like in her spiritual nature, and to Whom she is not less like in will, loving as she is loved by Him. Thus, if she loves perfectly, she is a spouse. What is more sweet than this conformity of wills? What is more desirable than this love by which, O soul, discontented with the teachings of men, you are made to approach the Word with confidence, to stay united to Him, to dwell familiarly near Him, to consult Him in everything; so bold in your desire to know, that you feel yourself, through your intelligence, capable of possessing the knowledge. It is truly spiritual, truly holy, this contract of marriage: to speak of a contract is to say too little; it is a loving embrace. A veritable loving embrace, in which an identification of wills makes two spirits but one.'[6]

The entire conformity of views, of feelings, of will, that St Bernard depicts here is only possible because the soul, in all things, 'lets herself be directed by the Word': *Verbo se regere* ...

(*Sponsa Verbi, V*)

[1] 2 Cor. 11:2
[2] 'Or her sponsors renounce for her, until the time she ratifies their act deliberately' (Marmion's note).
[3] Psalm 118(119):53
[4] John 17:1
[5] Bossuet, *Meditations on the Gospel.*
[6] *On the Song of Songs*, 83.

12. HEAVEN IN THE SOUL

Written in August 1906, for Sœur Marie-Xavier de Jésus, for whom Elizabeth chose the name *Abscondita*, Hidden one.

Within Your sacred breast
          I would that I might flow,
A drop of water, lost
          in such a mighty sea!
Grant, all that's not divine
          destroy in me, that so
Into Your Being, swift
          my soul can then rush free.

A truly 'spacious place'
          I must seek entrance to! –
Unsoundable Abyss,
          those depths of Mystery;
To love You, Jesus, *as*
          in Heav'n they're loving You;
With nothing from outside
          to be distracting me.

I want to dwell within
          Your blazing hearth of love,
Beneath Your glorious Face –
          the radiance that it has! –
To live by You alone
          as in the Home Above,
In such delicious peace
          as nothing can surpass.

It's there that will occur
           the transformation! — there
That I shall, ah, become
           as if another You.
For that, O Beauty's height,
           there's one condition: dare
To give up all for You —
           that's what I here must do!

Yes! of oneself one lives
           no longer, loving true —
For, to forget one's self
           is, then, a need one knows:
Until the one we love
           we finally win to,
Our hearts can not relax,
           they do not have repose.

So, Jesus, with the love
           I have for You, that's why
My only need is *You* —
           Your Presence — ev'ry day!
Each second, sacrifice
           unseen but to Your eye.
In silence. From myself
           I want to go away.

Then bury me within
        tranquillity so deep —
Your Being, Infinite:
        that I (though here below)
May live as if in Heav'n;
        whatever comes, may keep
Your peace unbounded: joy
        at being chosen so.

In seeking for You — no,
        I've not to look outside
To find You to adhere
        to You! — it isn't this.
No! in my deepest heart
        I've only got to hide,
To lose myself, for good
        in what Your Essence is.

Last stanza: Literally, Elizabeth says that it is not a question of adhering to God
'substance to substance' but rather of losing herself for ever in God.

Elizabeth as a young pianist.

Notes

P 109

August 1906

> 'Then, bury me within
> tranquillity so deep –
> Your Being, Infinite . . .'

'O Eternal Word, Utterance of my God, I wish to spend my life in listening to You, I wish to make myself wholly teachable, so as to learn everything from You. Then, throughout all darkness, all emptiness, all helplessness, I wish to fix my gaze on You always and to live beneath Your great light. O my beloved Star! fascinate me, that I may no longer be able to go out of Your radiance.' (Elizabeth, Prayer to the Trinity)

It 'is of vital importance for the modern retreatant, retiring into himself and discovering what manner of man he is, to go back further and further into the tradition of the Church in order to plant his ladder securely on the sure ground of Gospel teaching before beginning to climb.' . . . Those who 'after making some gesture to God think immediately that they are holy, are misled by a false sun.' (Conrad Pepler, OP, *The English Religious Heritage*)

'The transformation . . . is a gradual process. Sins and weaknesses still remain; indeed the sinfulness of a man will often urge him on, increasing his thirst for our Lord until he is renewed. The more of Jesus he finds in his soul the more desire he has to find Jesus wholly and the more he despises the naught of his own sinfulness still remaining.' (Pepler, *ibid.*)

'He dwells in your soul and He wishes you to withdraw there with Him, so as to love and adore Him' (Elizabeth, letter to her mother, 19 June 1906).

BLESSED COLUMBA MARMION: Contemplation

When a soul is thus faithful in following Christ Jesus step by step, in letting itself be permeated by the Holy Spirit with truths from on high and in conforming its life to them, God leads it, little by little, to the *state* of prayer. There one has the third stage: that of the unitive life, where the soul attaches itself solely to God, to Christ. It is able to make its own the words of the Apostle: 'Who then shall separate us from the love of Christ?'[1] There are a good many degrees in this state, but it is certain that the day will come when God will raise us to the degree which is fitting for each of us, if we remain generously faithful in seeking only Him: 'I am thy protector, and thy reward exceeding great.'[2]

In the measure, indeed, that the soul strips itself of self, God acts more and more in it; He draws to Him all the faculties of the soul, in order to simplify the exercise of them. Prayer becomes more simple, the soul no longer feels the need of much reflection, of much thought, of much speaking; the direct action of God becomes more profound, the soul is before God, as it were, motionless, knowing that He is there, intimately united with Him by an act of loving adhesion, even though this act is enveloped in the darkness of faith. One might compare this union to that of two souls who know what each other thinks without any speaking, and are in a complete union of feelings without having any need to express them. Such is contemplation: the soul looks at God, loves Him and is silent. And God looks at that soul, and fills it to the brim. This is what persons do who are united in a deep love: when they have said everything, they are silent and gaze at each other: in that silent gaze all their love is gathered up, all their tenderness is conveyed. The soul remains in this prayer of faith, united to God, to Christ Jesus, without any intermediary interposing between them and it. The soul, as it were, puts on one side everything that the senses, natural intelligence, revealed symbols even, say of God, so as to repose in pure faith ...

In this rendezvous of the soul with its God, in this direct contact with the Beloved, the soul delivers itself up and it finds all its good; for God also communicates Himself to the soul, in revealing Himself. This contact of faith and of love is sometimes very short, lasts only a few moments, but it suffices to fill the soul with lights; the love of God becomes its own love, the Divine activity transforms its own activity.

This union with God in faith is very simple but very fruitful. For the soul who lives in it there is realized the saying of the Lord in Scripture: 'And I will espouse thee to Me in faith: and thou shalt know that I am the Lord.'[3] What ought the soul to do? Deliver itself up, let itself be taken; God touches the soul, takes hold of all its fibres in order to bring them back to Him, as to their centre; it is a Divine embrace, in which the soul, despite the aridities that can occur, despite the darkness, despite its powerlessness, ought to deliver itself up to the hand of the Divine Artist so as to let itself be transfigured.

The fruitfulness of this prayer merits for it the name of transforming. It is said that in heaven we shall be 'like to' God, 'because we shall see Him as He is'.[4] As soon as the blest soul sees God, it identifies itself with Him, in the intelligence by truth and in the will by love. To the extent that it is possible, the soul will be − not equal, obviously − but like to God: the Beatific Vision brings about this transformation, of making the soul like to God, to the point of being united with Him in unity. Now, what is it that, during this life, is for us a prelude to the vision of the elect? Prayer in faith. The soul, in contemplating God by faith, in prayer, sees His perfections and all truth; it delivers itself up to this truth; and thus seeing in God the sovereign Good, the only Good, its will unites itself to this Divine will, source for the soul of every bliss: and the more powerful that adhesion is, the more the soul is united to God. That is why prayer in faith is so precious for the soul. We ought to want to arrive at a high degree in this prayer; that is to say, to attain to that very simple and love-filled union with God, which results from an effusion of purest Divine light. The worth of this union is very great; for it sometimes transforms a soul in a very short time. Plunge an iron bar into the fire; the iron will not be long in sharing all the qualities of the fire. God is a furnace; the soul that plunges itself in God through prayer is wholly filled with light and with heat, its love increases by immense proportions, and one has there a choice grace. At this time God acts in the soul much more than the soul itself acts. God works in it, the Holy Spirit takes it in hand. One accomplishes at this time with great facility and much better what previously one did very imperfectly. God Himself produces the virtues for the acquisition of which we have laboured painfully in the past. This state is therefore exceedingly desirable; the Fathers have always regarded it as perfection, the normal crowning of the whole spiritual life. Far from producing pride, it makes there arise in the soul a most deep sense of its nothingness, for it is impossible for a creature to understand the greatness of God without grasping at the same time its own littleness.

However, it would be an error to believe that one can arrive at a high degree of this prayer without having laboured much and suffered much for God and His glory. In the ordinary conditions of His providence, God only gives Himself to the soul in such fullness in the evening of life, when the soul has proved, by a constant fidelity to the inspirations of grace, that it belongs wholly to God and that in all things it truly seeks but Him alone: 'whether he is truly seeking God'.[5]

(*Christ, the Ideal of the Monk*, XV.vi)

[1]   Rom. 8:35.
[2]   Gen. 15:1.
[3]   Hosea (Osee) 2:20.
[4]   1 John 3:2.
[5]   Rule of St Benedict, Ch. 53.

13. THE LAWS OF LOVE

Written for St Martha's Day, 1905. Elizabeth and Sœur Agnès, together that day in the kitchen, had the intention of working as though they were Martha and Mary welcoming Jesus at Bethany.

To love! It's when, in Carmel, you
Give *your*self up, like Jesus! For
Unhesitating love-that's-true
Wants always to be giving more.
Let us a faithful image be
(Our Spouse, atoning for us, died):
Within us trace our Model; He
Is God and He was crucified.

To love! Forgetting self, as did
The Angel of Lisieux: to be
Consumed, in (where her self was hid)
Her Loved One's burning fervency.
Thérèse had understood within;
Her great simplicity could tell.
His strong Love-message entered in:
'Come here, to my own Heart to dwell.'

To love! Like Mary Magdalene,
Her *being there* with Him: the way
She rested at His feet, serene
Before the Saviour . . . There she'd stay.
She listened all in silence when
His teaching made her spirit full.
(To savour more His presence then,
Her being spoke no syllable.)

To love! It means Apostles, bold
For God – who for His honour fight;

It is that heritage of old
Left to us by our Beacon-Light:
As Saint Teresa saw, and she
Gives it to us . . . a glimpse there came
Of what God's Home and Hearth may be —
Her Carmel was a furnace-flame.

To love! To be like Mary: hear
Her praises of God's greatness ring —
Magnificat; up-rising, clear
Her joy to Him we hear her sing.
Ah, self-annihilation is
Your centre, Mary! He abides
In faithful *lowliness*. In this
Eternal Splendour rests and hides.

To love is this — that Christ the King
Will find, for witness to Him, us
To pledge our life, our everything —
Our affirmation's greater thus.
Oh, like the martyrs of Compiègne,
With *our* blood be the ground bedewed!
And may the song we're singing then
Be wholly one of gratitude.

To 'praise His glory', always — may
Our self-oblation be complete;
To gain the vict'ry on the day,
God asks of us that we compete!
Our Mothers' zeal of old in mind —
Their fervour be to us a spur —
We'll leave our miseries behind:
Our Lord and King the Conqueror!

The translation is of the poem as published in the *Souvenirs*. For copyright reasons, I do
not include another stanza, and additional lines in each of these stanzas, which make the
poem twice as long as this. The poem refers to Sister (now Saint) Thérèse of Lisieux in
stanza 2, and to Saint Teresa of Avila in stanza 4.

P 94

29 July 1905

'Give yourself up, like Jesus!'

Some 'would like to reduce Thee, O my God, to a mere abstract idea, a vain word without meaning, a vague and impersonal thing: and behold, Thou revealest Thyself as being not only personal as we see that we ourselves are, but thrice Personal . . . our dealings with Thee, O my God, must, on our own part, be personal, most intimate and loving.' (Louismet, *The Burning Bush*)

'I have today had the joy of offering to my Jesus several sacrifices over my dominant fault, but how much they cost me! I recognize there my weakness. It seems to me that when I receive an unjust comment I feel the blood boil in my veins; all my being revolts! But Jesus was with me, I heard His voice in the depths of my heart, and then I was ready to bear anything for love of Him!' (Elizabeth, at age 18; her diary, 30 January 1899)

The Carmelite 'loves the Master so much . . . her life becomes like a continual gift of herself, an exchange of love with Him . . .' (Elizabeth, letter to Germaine de Gemeaux, 20 May 1903)

BLESSED COLUMBA MARMION: Love responding to Love

Love is active: of its nature it is overflowing. In Jesus, it can but have been for us an inexhaustible source of gifts.

In the prayer for the Feast of the Sacred Heart, the Church invites us to 'call to mind the principal benefits we owe to the love of Christ Jesus'. This contemplation is one of the elements of devotion to the Sacred Heart. How can one esteem a love when one does not know its manifestations?

This love, as we have said, is the human love of Jesus, a revelation of the uncreated love. To this uncreated love, love in common with the Father and the Holy Spirit, we owe everything. There is no gift which does not find in that love its deepest principle. What has drawn our beings out of nothing? Love. In the hymn for the Feast we sing: 'the earth, the sea, the stars, are the work of love' ...

Even more than creation, the Incarnation is due to love. 'It is that which made the Word come down from the splendours of the heavens to unite Himself with a nature weak and mortal.' ...

But the benefits of which we ought to remind ourselves above all are the Redemption through the Passion, the institution of the Sacraments – the Eucharist above all. It is to the human love of Jesus as much as to His uncreated love that we owe them ...

This contemplation of the benefits of Jesus in regard to us ought to become the source of our practical devotion to the Sacred Heart. Only love can respond to love. Of what does Our Lord complain to St Margaret Mary? Of not seeing His love repaid. 'Behold this heart that has so loved men, and that receives from them only ingratitude.' It is, then, through love, through the gift of our heart, that one must respond to Christ Jesus. 'Who would not love one who loves him? What ransomed one would not attach himself to his redeemer?'[1]

To be perfect, this love ought to bear a double character.

There is affective love; it consists of the different feelings which stir the soul in regard to a person loved: admiration, taking pleasure in the person; joy, thanksgiving. This love begets praise from our lips. We rejoice at the perfections of the heart of Jesus, we celebrate its beauty and its greatness, we take pleasure in the magnificence of its benefits: 'My lips shall greatly rejoice, when I shall sing to thee!'[2]

This affective love is necessary. When it contemplates Christ in His love, the soul ought to let itself go in its admiration, pleasure, jubilation. Why is that? Because we ought to love God with all our being; God wants our love for Him to correspond to our nature ...

Our love ought to burst forth in affection. Look at the Saints. Francis, the poor man of Assisi, was so transported with love that he sang the praises of God on the roads; Magdalen of Pazzi ran through the cloisters of her convent crying 'O love, O love!'. St Teresa thrilled, all over, every time she sang these words of the Creed: 'and His kingdom will have no end' ...

Let us, then, not be afraid of multiplying our praises directed to the heart of Jesus. Litanies, acts of reparation, of consecration, are so many expressions of this love of the feelings, without which the human soul does not reach the perfection of its nature.

By itself, this affective love is insufficient, however. For it to have its full value, it ought to 'translate itself into works'.[3] 'If you love me', said Jesus Himself, 'you will keep my commandments'.[4] That is the only touchstone. You will meet souls who abound in affection, who have the gift of tears – and who do not bother the least bit in the world to repress their bad inclinations, to destroy their habits of vice, to avoid the occasions of sin; who give way immediately temptation arises, or murmur as soon as annoyances or contradictions present themselves. With these people, affective love is full of illusion; it is a fire of straw that does not last, that disappears into ashes.

If we truly love Christ Jesus, not only will we rejoice in His glory, sing of His perfections with every impulse of our soul, be sad at the injuries done to His heart and offer amends to Him – but above all we will strive to obey Him in all things, we will accept with alacrity all the dispositions of His Providence in our regard, will employ ourselves in extending His reign in souls, in bringing Him glory; we 'gladly will spend' and if necessary go so far as to 'be spent' oneself, according to the beautiful words of St Paul.[5] The apostle says that about charity towards our neighbour;

applied to our love for Jesus, this formula sums up marvellously the practice of devotion to His Sacred Heart.

(Christ in His Mysteries, XIX.iii)

[1] Hymn of Lauds for the Feast of the Sacred Heart.
[2] Psalm 70 (71): 23.
[3] St Gregory, Homily on the Gospel, 30.1.
[4] John 14:15 (Jerusalem).
[5] 2 Cor. 12:15.

Mother Germaine.

14. THE DREAM OF A 'PRAISE OF GLORY'

In this poem, written in 1906 for the patronal feast-day of the Prioress, Mother Germaine, Elizabeth recognises the Prioress's great charity towards her, the love she showed in preparing her for 'the divine Rendezvous' from the time of her entry into the Carmel.

Note, however, that the love of the members of the Community for each other, admirable and edifying though it is, does not represent the whole of an enclosed nun's radiating love for others. Later pages will indicate this.

> I dreamt it was my joy
>> (O gentle Shepherdess)
> Where Love Itself has Home
>> to fête you in the height:
> But 'Praise of Glory', still
>> on earth, can only guess
> What was this glimpse she had
>> of that abode of Light ...
> Yet: in the Father's house
>> (deep down in me I said)
> Within that Secret Place,
>> the Heart of God, I sense
> That, Mother, I on *you*
>> in turn might blessings shed! –
> This notion flooded me
>> with happiness immense.
>
> I never shall forget
>> those hours I spent with you:
> Your forming of me – for
>> the Rendezvous divine;

The plans, together made
            (no words for this will do),
My Spouse would tell me 'Come!' –
            I waiting for His sign.
He consecrated you
            to act in this as would
A *priest* in sacrifice:
            you'd offer me and raise
My being to His love,
            delivered up for good:
To be consumed by Him
            through all my nights and days.

And, Mother – you recall –
            the Stream of Life would flow
Along one channel, you,
            to find its course in me . . .
While I was *in your heart*,
            by faith communing, so
The tides were flooding forth
            to whelm me utterly.
At each new dawn (so deep
            the silence always) you'd
Approach to bring to me
            my Saviour and my Lord:

May He express to you
        the love, the gratitude
That in your little child –
        her deeps of heart – are stored.

If, yet, the linen-cloth
        God has not willed to tear
That I might shining out
        His hidden Beauty see,
At least I now by faith
        lift up the veil, and there
I live, along with Him
        in His eternity.
Then (deep the mystery!)
        I felt my Master say
That this, my dream of heart,
        was truly to occur.
And for my Mother now
        I do not cease to pray:
'Lord, make her rich in grace'
        is what I ask for her.

My guide, in all I've done
          since coming, has been she:
Its in her arms, then, I
          would fall asleep; to go
To gaze upon that Light
          which beams eternally —
To sing there my *Sanctus*
          that never end shall know!
If 'Praise of Glory', here
          on earth, has never found
The words to speak her heart
          in 'thank you's, yet above
A resonating lyre,
          my Mother, by its sound
Will bring you — certainly!
          her sweet refrain of love.

> 'My guide, in all I've done.'

'You know how grateful I am to you: no day passes without my praying for you. Oh, you see, I feel that all the treasures enclosed in the soul of Christ are mine; so I feel so rich, and with what happiness I come to draw from that source for all those I love and *who have done good to me.*' (Elizabeth, letter to Canon Angles, 11 September 1901; her emphasis).

BLESSED COLUMBA MARMION:
Love one another

In all the preceding pages, we have seen how faith in Jesus Christ, Son of God – a living, practical faith that finds expression, under the influence of love, in the tasks of life, that nourishes itself by the Eucharist and prayer – brings us by degrees to intimate union with Christ to the point of transforming us into Him.

But if we want this transformation of our life into that of Christ Jesus to be complete and true, to encounter no obstacle to its perfection, the love that we have for Our Lord must radiate around us and shine out upon all men. That is what St John points out to us when he sums up the whole Christian life in these words: 'And this is His commandment, that we should believe in the name of His Son Jesus Christ: and love one another'.[1]

I have shown you, up to now, how faith in Jesus Christ is exercised; it remains for me now to tell you how we shall carry out His precept of mutual love ...

When did St John hear this commandment that he makes

known to us? At the Last Supper. The day so ardently desired by Our Lord has arrived: 'With desire I have desired ...'[2]; He has eaten the pasch with His disciples; but He has replaced figures and symbols with a Divine reality; He has just instituted the Sacrament of union, and given His apostles the power of perpetuating it. And now it is that, before going to suffer death, He opens His Sacred Heart to reveal its secrets to His 'friends';[3] it is like the will and testament of Christ: 'A new commandment I give unto you: That you love one another, as I have loved you';[4] and at the end of His discourse He renews His precept: 'This is my commandment, that you love one another'[5] ...

Our Lord calls 'new' the precept of *Christian* charity, because it was something which had not been explicitly promulgated, at least in its universal acceptation, in the Old Testament. The precept of the love of God had been explicitly given in the Pentateuch; and love of God includes *implicitly* love of neighbour: some great saints of the Old Testament had understood, by the light of grace, that the duty of fraternal affection extended to the whole human race. But in no part of the Old Law does one find an *explicit* precept to love *all men* ... The explicit precept to love all men, including one's enemies, had not been affirmed and promulgated before Jesus Christ. That is why He calls it a 'new' precept and 'His' precept ...

So much is it His desire, that He makes it, not a counsel but a commandment, *His* commandment, and that He gives the fulfilment of it as the infallible sign by which one will recognize His disciples: 'By this shall all men know that you are My disciples, if you have love one for another'[6] ... the super-natural love that you will have for one another will be an unequivocal proof that you truly belong to Me. And, in fact, in the early centuries the pagans used to recognize Christians by this sign: 'Just see', they would say, 'how they love each other!'

For Our Lord himself, this will be the sign He will use on the day of judgement to distinguish the elect from the

145

reprobate; it is He who tells us that; listen to Him, for He is infallible Truth.

After the resurrection of the dead, the Son of Man will be seated on His throne of glory; the nations will be assembled before Him: He will place the good on His right hand and the wicked on His left. And, addressing the good: 'Come, ye blessed of my Father, possess you the kingdom prepared for you from the foundation of the world.' And what reason for it will He give: 'I was hungry, and you gave me to eat: I was thirsty, and you gave me to drink: I was a stranger, and you took me in: naked, and you covered me: sick, and you visited me: I was in prison, and you came to me.' And the just will be astonished, for they have never seen Christ in these necessities. But He will reply to them: 'Amen I say to you, as long as you did it to one of these my least brethren, you did it to me.'[7] ...

When we appear before Christ on the Last Day, He will not ask us if we have fasted much, if we have lived a life of penitence, if we have passed numerous hours in prayer – no, but if we have loved and assisted our brethren. Then is it that the other commandments are left on one side? Certainly not; but their fulfilment will have served for nothing if we have not observed this precept – so dear to Our Lord because it is *His* commandment – of loving one another.

On the other hand, it is impossible for a soul to be perfect in the love of neighbour without possessing in it the love of God; which love at the same time embraces within its whole scope the Divine will. Why is that?

The reason is that charity – whether it has God for its object or whether it is exercised in regard to one's neighbour – is *one* in its supernatural *motive*, which is the infinite perfection of God. That, then, is why if you truly love God, you will necessarily love your neighbour. 'Perfect charity towards neighbour', said the Eternal Father to St Catherine of Siena, 'essentially depends on the perfect charity one has for Me. The same measure of perfection or imperfection which the soul puts into its love for Me is met with again in the love it bears to creatures.' From another standpoint, there are so many causes that distance us from our neighbour: selfishness, conflicts of interest, differences of character, injuries received, that if you love your neighbour really and super-naturally it cannot but be that the love of God is reigning in your soul, and, with the love of God, the other virtues He commands. If you do not love God, your love of neighbour will not long resist the difficulties it will encounter in its exercise.

(*Christ, the Life of the Soul*, Part II, XI, opening section and i)

[1]   1 John 3:23.
[2]   Luke 22:15.
[3]   John 15:13–15
[4]   John 13:34.
[5]   John 15:12.
[6]   John 13:35.
[7]   Matt. 25:40.

15. MY CRUCIFIED LOVE

Elizabeth identifies with Christ, not only in the performance of the 'Work of God' in the Carmel, but in being willing – if it is the Divine will – to accept sufferings in order to save souls in union with Him.

In the first stanza Elizabeth quotes from Blessed Angela of Foligno.

About her Master once
                a holy woman said:
'If not in Sorrow, where? –
                tell me, where does He dwell?'
I want to raise His Cross
                high, up above my head,
So, I (O Mother – 'Priest')
                wish to live there as well.

But I have need of you,
                the shadow of your wing,
Then, I can ingress make
                into that fortress strong –
Into that citadel,
                that palace of the King
Where peace invincible,
                repose-of-soul, belong.

148

David said this, of Christ:
              'Immense His sorrow'. So
What else should be my home
              but this immensity?
A sacrifice, *I* will
              in holy silence go
That I may be transformed —
              of Love, a 'victim' be.

Notes

P 113

14 September 1906

> 'What else should be my home
> but this immensity?'

'The soul that wants to serve God night and day in His temple – I mean that interior sanctuary of which St Paul speaks when he says: "The temple of God is sacred, and you are that temple" (1 Cor. 3:17)[1] – this soul has to resolve to be in *effective* communion with the Passion of its Master. She is a ransomed one who must ransom other souls in her turn, and for that she will sing on the lyre: "I glory in the cross of Jesus Christ. With Christ I am nailed to the cross." (Gal. 6:14; 2:19). And again: "I . . . fill up those things that are wanting of the sufferings of Christ, in my flesh, for His Body, which is the Church" (Col. 1:24) . . . she walks the way of Calvary at the right hand of her crucified King . . . He wishes to associate His spouse with His work of redemption . . .' (Elizabeth, *Last Retreat*, Fifth Day).

BLESSED COLUMBA MARMION: Ambassadors within the walls.

> I was saying to you in the preceding discussion[2] that, in choir [Marmion is speaking of the devout recitation of the Divine Office], we are the ambassadors of the Church. Now, what is the most fundamental quality for an ambassador? To be skilful? powerful? to have at his disposal a big fortune? to command belief? to shine by his personal talents? to be *persona grata* with the sovereign to whom he is sent? All that is useful, necessary; all these qualities will contribute without any doubt to the success of what he does, but they will be insufficient and sterile, will even deviate from the end sought, if the ambassador does not in

the first place identify himself in the most perfect possible way, with the intentions and the feelings of the sovereign who sends him, with the interests of the country he represents. Now, the Church deputes us [monks and nuns] to the King of kings, to the throne of God. We ought, then, to identify ourselves with His views and His wishes; the Church entrusts to us her interests, which are those of souls, those of eternity. This is not a trivial matter! Let us then take into our hearts all the needs, all the necessities of the Church (so dear to Jesus, since it is bought at the price of His Blood), the anguish of souls who are in pain, the perils of those who at this moment are grappling with the devil, the solicitude of those who have to direct us; in order that each of these may receive the help of God. This is what a holy Benedictine nun, Sister Mechtilde of Magdeburg, did: she took Christendom into the arms of her soul to present it to the Eternal Father, in order that it might be saved. 'Leave it', cried the Lord, 'it is too heavy for you!'. 'No, Lord', replied the saint, 'I want to lift it up so as to carry it to Your feet, to Your own arms, in order that thus You may carry it Yourself upon the cross.' ...

It is true that worldly people shrug their shoulders when they learn that that we stay long hours in choir to praise God. For them, nothing has worth except what is exterior, what one can touch or finger the results of; what one talks about, what has been successful, what dazzles one ... [But] it is during these hours that we carry out apostolic work par excellence, even in regard to our neighbour: for him we obtain help from on high, the grace of God, we give him God: this is a soul's greatest good.

(*Christ, the Ideal of the Monk*, XIV.iv)

---

[1]   Jerusalem.
[2]   Earlier in this section of *Christ, the Ideal of the Monk*

16. HYMN TO SUFFERING

Elizabeth wrote a seven-stanza poem in April 1898, a little over three years before she entered Carmel. The three stanzas below are those published in the *Souvenirs*.

Stab, stab now, O you dear Suffering,
Stab, stab! my dear one, Pain and Woe:
Be you my hope while I'm here below —
For the Saviour was not spared your sting.

Stab — for I can't live without you! Be
Here, so that Jesus may look and see
Me in His image . . . one crucified
Who drinks of the cup with Him who died.

Stab! for it's joy I am welcoming —
What trial and sacrifice can bring:
My hope is for these to play their part
Now in consoling my Loved One's heart.

Notes

P 46

8 April 1898

'Stab, stab now, O you dear Suffering.'

'Oh! how beautiful to contemplate she [the Blessed Virgin] is
during her long martyrdom – so serene, enveloped in a sort of
majesty that breathes at the same time strength and gentleness. It
is that she has learned from the Word Himself how they should
suffer, those whom the Father has chosen as victims, those whom
He has resolved to associate with the great work of redemption,
those whom He has known and "predestined to be made
conformable to the image of His Son" (Rom. 8:29), crucified by
love' (Elizabeth, *Last Retreat*, Fifteenth Day).

'Think of it, then – (my) sharing in the sufferings of my cruci-
fied Spouse, and going with Him to my passion to be a
redemptrix with Him ...' (Elizabeth, letter to her mother,
18 July 1906).

BLESSED COLUMBA MARMION:
Embracing the cross

To those who are more 'advanced in faith and in obser-
vance'[1] – who, by Christ's grace, have already acquired the
strength to break free of bad tendencies so as to 'run in the
way of the commandments',[2] St Benedict presents another
motive, a higher one and not less powerful: sharing in the
sufferings of Christ. Indeed, for faithful and holy souls, who
have made satisfaction for their faults, whose union with
God is more assured against the assaults of the enemy,
renouncement of oneself becomes the means and the proof
of a more perfect imitation of Our Lord. These souls volun-
tarily embrace the cross so as to 'aid' Christ in His Passion:

Calvary is the preferred place to which Love draws and keeps them ...

We find in a letter of St Paul words which, at first sight, seem astonishing: I 'rejoice in my sufferings for you, and fill up those things that are wanting of the sufferings of Christ, in my flesh, for His body, which is the Church.'[3] What do these words mean? Do the sufferings of Christ, then, lack something? Oh! no; we know that in themselves they have been, so to say, measureless: measureless in their intensity, for they swept down like a torrent on Christ to submerge him; measureless above all in their worth, a worth in the precise sense infinite ... Christ, having died for all, is become, by His Passion 'the propitiation' for the sins 'of the whole world'.[4]

That being so, what is the meaning of this text of the Apostle? St Augustine explains it to us. To understand the mystery of Christ, one must not separate Him from His Mystical Body; Christ, according to the expression of the great Doctor, is the 'whole' Christ only if one takes Him as *united to* the Church; He is the Head of the Church which forms His Mystical Body. Hence, Christ having given His share of the expiation, it remains to His Mystical Body to bring its own share too ... A soul that truly loves Our Lord wishes to give Him, by its mortifications, this proof of its love for His Mystical Body. Therein we find the secret of the 'extravagances' of the saints, of that thirst for mortifications which characterises nearly all of them: to 'fill up those things that are wanting' of the Passion of their Divine Master ...

Because He stayed fastened to the cross through love, He gave to His Father infinite glory, worthy of the Divine perfections. We, too – we fastened ourselves to the cross on the day of our profession: we did it through love; and if we stay faithful to our post of immolation, it is still through love. That does not prevent nature from feeling pain. You say to me: is not the monastery the ante-chamber of heaven? Assuredly; but to live for a long time in a place of waiting, and to live there in monotony, amid things that annoy, can become singularly burdensome and call for a large dose of endurance.

We ought, nevertheless, to hold firm and be patient until God's good time: 'Do manfully ... and wait thou for the Lord'.[5] God is never so near to us as when He places the cross of His Son on our shoulders; never more than in those same moments do we give return to our Heavenly Father of the glory He derives from our patience: 'they ... bring forth fruit in patience'[6] ...

(Christ, the Ideal of the Monk, IX.i–iii)

---

[1]   Prologue to Rule of St Benedict
[2]   *Ibid*; cf. Psalm 118 (119):32
[3]   Col. 1:24.
[4]   1 John 2:2.
[5]   Psalm 26 (27):14.
[6]   Luke 8:15.

17. RENDEZVOUS OF LAUDEM GLORIAE WITH HER DEAR SISTER

The recipient of this poem was Sœur Marie-Xavier de Jésus. The 'two-fold abyss' is the abyss of God's immensity and the abyss of man's nothingness (Blessed Angela of Foligno).

A private rendezvous
        I make with you. It's this —
So secret and divine,
        mysterious! . . . it's where
We ought to hide, and deep
        in that two-fold abyss:
The gentle peace of Heav'n
        we'll be awaiting, there.

Go down! Let's always learn
        to find the lowest place:
To be like Him, our Spouse,
        that is the way one goes.
And then will shine on us
        the glory of His Face;
To humble ones He's drawn —
        to gentle ones. To those.

In order that we can
        live with Him always — well,
There's a condition: I
        must being to naught the 'me'.
Abasement of the self! —
        let this be where we dwell,
Our royal palace: this
        our habitation be.

Statue of Our Lady in the Dijon Carmel.

Notes

P 120

3rd October 1906

'So secret and divine . . .'

'He wishes to be my peace so that nothing may be able to distract me or make me go out from "the impregnable fortress of holy recollection" [St John of the Cross]. There He will give me "access to the Father" and will keep me motionless and peaceful in His presence, as if my soul were already in eternity. It is by the Blood of His Cross that He will bring peace to everything in my little heaven, in order that it may truly be the repose of the Three . . .' (Elizabeth, *Last Retreat*, Twelfth Day)

'Give peace to my soul, make it Your heaven, Your beloved dwelling and the place of Your repose. May I never leave You there alone, but be wholly present, wholly awake in my faith, wholly adoring, wholly yielded up to Your creative Action.' (Elizabeth, Prayer to the Trinity)

'Abide in God in the secret place of your soul . . . What is more blessed than to cast all our care on Him who cannot fail? As long as you lean upon yourself you will totter. Throw yourself without fear into the arms of God . . .' (Blessed Albert the Great, *On Union with God*).

'However, this perfect quiet is not the death of the mind but its true life. "Instead of bringing darkness and torpor, the sleep of the Spouse is wakeful and life-giving . . ." [St Bernard]. This perfect tranquillity of mind, in which we enjoy the loving God by returning His love, and by which we turn and direct ourselves and all we have to Him, does not reduce us to laziness, sloth and inertia, but awakens an assiduous, efficient and active zeal that spurs us on to procure our own salvation and, with the help of God, that of others also.' (Pius XII, Encyclical letter, *Doctor Mellifluus*)

BLESSED COLUMBA MARMION:
The Peace of Christ

When Christ appeared on earth, after so many thousands of years of waiting and of anguish, what was the first message that came down from heaven, the message in which men could discover in advance the secret of the ineffable mystery of the Word Incarnate, and which was like a programme of the whole of the work of Jesus? It was the one made heard by the angels sent by God himself to announce to the world the good news of the coming of His Son. 'Glory to God in the highest: and on earth peace to men of good will.'[1] The Word is made flesh to give all glory to His Father and bring peace to the world. The seeking of the Father's glory sums up, has within it, all the aspirations of the Heart of Christ in regard to Him who sent Him and whose beloved Son He is; the gift of interior peace condenses in itself all the good things the Saviour brings here below to the souls He comes to redeem.

Christ's life on earth has no other objective: when it is attained, Jesus regards His work as finished. Listen to what He says to His Father in the presence of His apostles, in that wonderful prayer spoken out loud, at the moment when He is about to consummate His life by His sacrifice: 'I have glorified Thee on the earth; I have finished the work which Thou gavest Me to do.'[2] And at that same moment, what does He say to His disciples to show them that, in their regard also, He has 'finished His work'? He leaves them peace, His own peace; not that which the world promises, but that which He alone can give.[3] It is the perfect gift that He leaves to His apostles, as to all souls redeemed and saved.

This good thing is so precious and so necessary for the preservation of other good things, that Jesus lays down that a wish for this peace shall be the normal greeting His disciples shall give on approaching someone.[4] Look at St Paul, herald par excellence of the mystery of Christ: all his letters[5] begin with this greeting: 'Grace to you, and peace from God our Father, and from the Lord Jesus Christ.' The apostle associates grace with peace, because grace is the first condition for peace: 'without grace', says St Thomas, 'there cannot be true peace' ...

Our heart is created for God ... our heart is infinite in its capacity, and no created being is able to satisfy it perfectly.

(Christ, *the Ideal of the Monk*, XVIII, opening section and i)

1 Luke 2:14.
2 John 17:4.
3 John 14:27.
4 Luke 10:5.
5 'Except that to the Hebrews the material redaction of which, as we know, was probably not by Paul's own hand' (Marmion's note).

Elizabeth, in the garden of the Carmel, in early 1903.

18. ALWAYS BELIEVE IN LOVE

Elizabeth wrote this in 1905 for the patronal feast-day of Sœur
Marie-Dominique, an extern sister.

Dear little garden-flower —
        stay, Sister, all your days
(Stay in this mystic patch)
        beneath the Heavenly gaze:
Let it imprint on you —
        firm as a seal is pressed
A radiancy of light,
        the Face of Christ your Blest.
Be as a crystal pure
        where the Divinity,
Reflected there in you,
        will His own Beauty see.
When you observe no more
        His sweet flame burn as bright,
When, rather, is your soul
        covered with deepest night,
Yet still believe in Love —
        that is the torch, to send
Light, that your steps may reach
        the Object-without-end.
Sister, we can! By faith
        the heart's-desire is found:
Simply repose in Him,
        touch Him and clasp Him round!

Now, on your feast-day's eve
　　　　(for you, as its bouquet),
Of Jesus in His love
　　　　I'm asking this: I pray
That He may make you rich,
　　　　may grant in high degree
Faith like *the faith of saints*
　　　　which, fixed on God, will see –
Through all things that befall –
　　　　the action of His love.
By faith we live on earth,
　　　　dear to the Lord above.

Notes

P 95

4 August 1905

'Always believe in Love.'

'Jesus said to me "My Divine Heart is . . . full of love for men, and for you in particular . . ." After these words, our Lord asked her for her heart. She begged of Him to take it. This He did, and placed it in His own Adorable Heart, where He showed it to her as a little atom which was being consumed in this burning furnace . . .' (Life of St Margaret Mary)

'If you have to suffer, think that you are even *more loved* still, and sing your thanks always . . .' (Elizabeth, letter to her sister, Guite, end of April 1906)

BLESSED COLUMBA MARMION: The Heart of Christ

Everything we possess in the domain of grace comes to us from Christ Jesus: 'of his fulness we have all received.'[1] He has destroyed the wall of separation which prevented us from going to God; He has merited all graces for us in infinite abundance; Divine Head of the Mystical Body, He possesses the power of communicating to us the spirit of His interior states and the virtue of His mysteries, in order to transform us into Him.

When we consider these mysteries of Jesus, which one of His perfections is it that we there see shining forth to us in particular? It is love.

Love brought about the Incarnation: 'For us . . . He came down from heaven . . . and became man';[2] it is love that makes Christ be born in a flesh capable of suffering and feeble; that inspires the obscurity of His hidden life; that nourishes the zeal of His public life. If Jesus delivers Himself up to death for us, it is because He yields to the excess of a measureless love;[3] if He rises from the dead, it is 'for our justification';[4] if He ascends to heaven, it is as one going before to 'prepare a place' for us[5] in that habitation of bliss. He sends 'the Spirit, the Consoler' so as not to 'leave us orphans';[6] He institutes the sacrament of the Eucharist as a memorial of His love.[7] All these mysteries have their source in love.

It is necessary that our faith in this love of Christ Jesus be lively and constant. And why? Because it is one of the most powerful supports of fidelity.

Look at St Paul: never was there a man who toiled, who spent himself, as he did for Christ. One day when his enemies attack the legitimacy of his mission, he is brought, in order to defend himself, to sketch out his own picture of his works, his labours and his sufferings. This picture – one of such vividness – you doubtless know; but it is always a joy to the soul to re-read that page, one unique in the annals of the apostolate. Often, says the great apostle, I have seen death near at hand; five times I have suffered the ordeal of flagellation; three times I was beaten with rods; once they stoned me; three times I was shipwrecked; I passed a day and a night in the depths of the sea. And my number-less journeys, full of perils: perils on rivers, perils from brig-ands, perils from people of my own nation, from the faithless; perils in towns, in deserts, perils at sea; my labours and my sufferings, my numerous night-watches; the tortures of hunger and thirst, the multiple fasts, the cold, the nakedness: and without speaking of so many other things still, let me recall my every-day cares, the solicitude I had for all the churches I founded.[8] Elsewhere, he applies to himself the words of the Psalmist: 'For thy sake ... we face death at every moment, reckoned no better than sheep marked down for slaughter ...' And yet, what does he add straight away? 'Yet in all this we are conquerors'.[9]

And where does one find the secret of this victory? Ask

him why he bears with everything, even 'weariness of living'[10] – why, in all his trials, he stays united to Christ with a steadfastness so unshakeable that neither tribulation, nor distress, nor persecution, nor hunger, nor the sword can separate him from Jesus?[11] He will answer you: 'Because of Him that hath loved us.'[12] What supports him, fortifies him, animates him, stimulates him, is the deep conviction of the love that Christ bears for him: He 'loved me, and delivered Himself for me'.[13]

And, indeed, the sentiment to which this ardent conviction gives birth within him is that he 'wishes no longer to live for himself' – he who has blasphemed the name of God and persecuted the Christians – but for Him who has loved him to the point of giving His life for him. '*Caritas Christi urget me . . .*' 'Christ's love urges me on', he exclaims.[14] That is why he would deliver himself up for Him, gladly spend himself, without reserve, without counting the cost; exhaust himself for the souls that are His conquest: 'I most gladly will spend and be spent myself.'[15]

This conviction, that Christ loves him, gives the real key to all the work of the great apostle.

Nothing impels us more towards love than the knowledge and the feeling of being loved. 'Every time we think about Jesus Christ', says St Teresa, 'let us recall the love by which He has showered us with benefits . . . Love calls forth love'.[16]

But how are we to know of this love which underlies all the interior states of Jesus, which explains them and sums up all His motives? from where are we to draw this science, so salutary and so fruitful that St Paul made it the object of his prayer for his Christians?[17] In contemplating the mysteries of Jesus. If we study them with faith, the Holy Spirit, who is Infinite Love, uncovers the depths of them and leads us to the love that is their source.

(*Christ in His Mysteries*, XIX, opening section)

---

1   John 1:16.
2   Nicene Creed.
3   John 13:1.

[4] Rom. 4:25.
[5] John 14:2; Hebr. 6:20.
[6] John 14:18.
[7] Luke 22:19.
[8] See 2 Cor. 11:23–28.
[9] Rom. 8:36–37; Psalm 43(44):23 (both Knox).
[10] See 2 Cor. 1:8 (Marmion's phrase, giving this reference, is *l'ennui de vivre*.)
[11] Rom. 8:35.
[12] Rom. 8:37.
[13] Gal. 2:20.
[14] See 2 Cor. 5:14.
[15] 2 Cor. 12:15.
[16] St Teresa of Avila, *Life*, Ch. 22.
[17] See Eph. 3:19.

19. WITH WHAT EXCESS OF LOVE!

A poem Elizabeth wrote for the fifth anniversary of the election of Mother Germaine as Prioress. Looking back to the day five years before, it is a grateful tribute to the love which the Prioress has shown towards her since then. The rhetorical reference to overflowing – French *trop* – echoes St Paul's phrase 'excess of love' (Eph. 2:4, Knox) with its overtones of a cup running over. Likened to and following that Divine 'excess', the Prioress's spiritual love for her is itself an element in God's plan for her, Elizabeth.

A further point of much interest lies in what the poem shows almost incidentally: the firm faith and hope that looks ahead to her own 'transfer' up to her 'Home above'. The poem was written in the Infirmary a month before her death: she knows she will die before the older woman, the Prioress.

> That day was God-ordained:
> > the Father, by decree,
> Laid down that you began
> > my Mother here to be.
> I hail that joyous day:
> > the Triune Loving – more,
> 'Excess of Charity'!
> > I see it, and adore.
>
> Such overflowing love! –
> > *that*'s what it is, I know,
> When God, in prescient love,
> > arranged that this be so –
> For He (that I should make
> > oblation here fore-known)
> Had consecrated you
> > with unction of His own.

And, from the very start,
           O Mother, God was pleased
To love as one in Him
           His victim and His priest:
His gaze of love on us
           from all eternity,
He'll always look and see
           not two, but unity.

So, if your little 'host'
           (O Pontiff, whom I love!)
Is very soon transferred
           up to the Home Above,
She will be yours still more! –
           I think it might be so –
Than when the night of faith
           she lived in, here below.

Have you not seen a priest
           who's going through the town
Carrying God, the Host,
           hidden beneath his gown? –
On your maternal heart
           that way, will not it be
That Laudem Gloriae
           spends her eternity?

Notes

P 122

9 October 1906

'His loving gaze on us
from all eternity . . .'

'David sang: "My soul longeth and fainteth for the courts of the Lord" (Psalm 83:1). It seems to me that this should be the attitude of every soul which returns to its interior courts to contemplate its God there . . .' (Elizabeth, *Last Retreat*, Sixteenth Day)

'O my Three, my All, my Beatitude, infinite Solitude, Immensity in which I lose myself, I deliver myself up to You as a prey. Bury Yourself in me, that I may bury myself in You, while waiting to go and contemplate in Your Light the abyss of Your greatness.' (Elizabeth, Prayer to the Trinity)

'The horizon is so beautiful!' (Elizabeth, letter to Canon Angles, 17 April 1902)

'. . . he no longer looks to heaven as though at a distant horizon. He knows by experience that heaven is the essence of his union, for it is that in which he communicates with God. He has found Love and he can look no further, only desiring that love may more and more drench his being': description of a soul in a high degree of union with God, on earth (Pepler, *The English Religious Heritage*)

BLESSED COLUMBA MARMION: Faith and Hope, and our eternal destiny

We must distinguish infused virtues from natural virtues. The latter are qualities, 'habits', that man, even an unbeliever, acquires and develops in himself by his personal efforts and his repeated acts: such as courage, strength,

170

prudence, justice, gentleness, loyalty, sincerity. These are natural dispositions that we have cultivated and which have arrived, by our exercise of them, at the state of acquired habits. They perfect and embellish our *natural* being in the intellectual or simply moral domain ...

Of another essence are the super-natural infused virtues. To begin with, they transport us above our nature. We exercise them no doubt by the faculties with which nature has endowed us (intelligence and will), but these faculties are heightened, raised right up, if I may so express it, to the divine level; in such a way that acts of these virtues reach the proportions requisite for attaining to our super-natural end. Then also, it is not by our personal efforts that we acquire them; but the germ of them is liberally placed within us by God with the grace in whose train they come: *They are poured together* ...

The Council of Trent, when it speaks of the increase of the divine life in us, distinguishes above all faith, hope and charity. They are called *theological*, because they have God as their immediate object; by them, we can know God, hope in Him, love Him in a super-natural way, worthy of our vocation to future glory and of our condition as God's children ...

What, indeed, is needed in order to possess God? One needs, to begin with, to *know* Him; in the life above we shall see Him face to face, and that is why 'we shall be like to Him: because we shall see Him as He is';[1] but here below we do not see Him; it is by *faith* in Him, in His Son, that we believe in His word, that we know Him; it is knowledge in obscurity. But what He tells us of Himself, of His nature, of His life, of His designs for redemption through His Son, we nevertheless know with certainty; the Word who is always in the bosom of the Father tells us what He sees, and we know it because we believe what He says: 'No man hath seen God at any time: the only-begotten Son who is in the bosom of the Father, He hath declared Him.'[2] This knowledge of faith is therefore a divine knowledge, and that is why Our Lord has said that it is a knowledge which brings eternal life: 'Now this is eternal life: that they may KNOW Thee, the only true God, and Jesus Christ, whom Thou hast sent.'[3]

In this light of faith, we know where our beatitude is; we know what 'eye hath not seen, nor ear heard, neither hath it entered into the heart of man' to conceive, namely the beauty and greatness of the glory that 'God hath prepared for them that love Him'.[4] But this ineffable beatitude is beyond the strength of our nature; shall we be able to get there? Yes, without any doubt; God even places in our soul this feeling that we are assured of reaching that supreme goal with His grace, the fruit of the merits of Jesus, and in spite of opposing obstacles. We can say with St Peter: 'Blessed be the God and Father of our Lord Jesus Christ, who according to His great mercy hath regenerated us (in baptism) unto a lively *hope*, by the resurrection of Jesus Christ from the dead, unto an inheritance incorruptible ... reserved in heaven' for us.'[5]

Finally, *charity*, love, brings about our drawing closer to God, here below, whilst waiting to possess Him up above. Charity completes and perfects faith and hope; it makes us experience a real taking of pleasure in God, we prefer God to everything, and we seek to manifest to God this taking of pleasure and this preference, by observing His will. 'The companion of faith', says St Augustine, 'is hope; hope is necessary because we do not see what we believe; with it, we do not fall faint in the waiting; indeed, charity comes and puts into our heart a hunger and thirst for God, imprints in our soul an impetus towards Him.'[6] For the Holy Spirit has shed in our hearts the charity which makes us cry out to God 'Father! Father!'. It is a super-natural faculty which makes us adhere to God as the infinite goodness we love more than anything else: 'Who then shall separate us from the love of Christ?'.[7]

(*Christ, the Life of the Soul*, Part II, VI.i–ii)

[1] 1 John 3:2.
[2] John 1:18.
[3] John 17:3.
[4] 1 Cor. 2:9.
[5] 1 Pet. 1:3–4.
[6] Sermon 53.
[7] Rom. 8:35.

Maredsous Abbey, Belgium, of which Marmion was abbot.

20. WE'LL EACH THE OTHER FIND WITHIN THE TRINITY

Elizabeth wrote this in the infirmary, just over three months before her death. It was written for the patronal feast-day of the Sister Infirmarian, Sœur Anne de Jésus, who had been looking after her.

Dear nurse, it's from the heart
    your little patient sings
Her 'thank-you's to you now.
    She's singing very low.
But, still, this feast-day prayer –
    like a bouquet – she brings
Upward, to God Himself
    for you, must surely go.
Maybe I very soon
    shall leave this world behind
To gaze on Beauty's self
    Unsayable! And yet
There, in the Father's house
    that you were here so kind –
How delicate your care! –
    these things I won't forget.
God gave to you for me
    a mother's goodness – yes,
I love you on my part
    just like a child would do.
Sister, when endless light
    as dwelling I possess,
You'll know how much my heart
    feels gratitude to you.
Out of the Fount of Life,
    its waters crystal-clear –

The river that flows out
             where is enthroned the Lamb,
Grace upon grace I'll draw,
             for you who are yet here:
I'll show how ever-glad
             in doing so I am.
We'll each the other find
             within the Trinity,
Of Whom we often talk
             (discussion that is sweet):
Beneath Its warm embrace,
             in Its immensity,
We two, though parted souls —
             we, nonetheless, can meet.
Communing, we with God —
             together doing this —
We — you and I — will not
             our separation feel,
But silently adore
             and know this as it is:
God, who unites us two,
             has put on that His seal.
The Father make you rich
             in blessing you. May He
Who is the Word of God
             imprint His image clear;
The Holy Spirit, love,
             consume you, ceaselessly —
This is the prayer she makes,
             your little sister here.

Notes

P 104

26 July 1906

'To gaze on Beauty's self, Unsayable!'

'A Dieu, beloved Sister, everything speaks to me of my departure for the Father's House; if you knew with what serene joy I am awaiting the face-to-face ...' (Elizabeth, letter to Clémence Blanc, July 1906)

Though 'in glory we shall see God face to face ... and see the Divine operations of the eternal generation of the Son and the eternal breathing out of the Holy Ghost, a mystery it will remain for evermore ... Only God can fathom God or understand or express Him fully. However, let us hasten to add that it were wrong to fancy that the happiness of the Blessed will, on this score, suffer any curtailment. On the contrary, this very fact of the absolute infinitude and incomprehensibleness of God will be to them a subject of joy and praise, for ever fresh and inexhaustible.' (Louismet, *The Burning Bush*)

'For the Trinity is God: God is the Trinity; the Trinity is our Maker and Keeper, the Trinity is our everlasting love and everlasting joy and bliss ...' (Mother Julian of Norwich)

BLESSED COLUMBA MARMION:
Fulfilment, in Heaven

Speaking of the theological virtues which come in the train of sanctifying grace and which are like sources of supernatural activity on the part of a child of God, St Paul says that in our present state, here below, 'there remain faith, hope, charity, these three'; but he adds: 'the greatest of these is charity'.[1] And what is the reason for that? Because in heaven, in the completion of our adoption, faith in God

176

gives place to the vision of God, hope vanishes in the possession of God, but love remains and unites us to God for ever.

This is what it consists in, the glorification that awaits us and which will be ours: we shall see God, we shall love God, we shall joy in God; these acts constitute eternal *life*, an assured and full participation in the very life of God; and hence beatitude of the soul, a beatitude in which the body is to share after the resurrection.

In heaven, we shall *see* God. To see God as He sees Himself is the first element of this participation in the Divine nature which constitutes the *life* of blessedness; it is the first vital act in glory. Here below, says St Paul, we only know God by faith, in an obscure manner, but then we shall see Him 'face to face': today, he says, I only know God imperfectly, but then I shall know Him 'even as I am known' by Him.[2] What it is in itself, this seeing, we cannot know now;[3] but the soul will be affirmed by 'the light of glory', which is nothing else but grace itself opening forth in heaven. We shall see God with all His perfections: or rather, we shall see that all His perfections come down to one infinite perfection which is Divinity; we shall contemplate the inner life of God; we shall enter, as St John says, into fellowship with the Holy and Blessed Trinity, Father, Son and Holy Spirit;[4] we shall contemplate the fullness of Being, the fullness of all truth, all holiness, all beauty, all goodness. We shall contemplate, and for ever, the humanity of the Incarnate Word; we shall see Christ Jesus, in whom the Father is infinitely well-pleased; we shall see Him who has willed to become our 'elder brother'; we shall contemplate the Divine features, henceforth glorious, of Him who has delivered us from death by the bloodshed of His Passion, who has given us to live this immortal life. It is to Him that we shall sing a hymn of thanksgiving: 'You it is who have ransomed us, O Lord, by your Blood; who have established us in Your kingdom: to You, praise and glory!'[5] We shall see the Virgin Mary, the choirs of angels,

177

all that multitude of the elect which St John declares unnumberable and whom he shows surrounding the throne of God.

This, that we see God without veil, without obscurity, without intermediary, is our future heritage, is the consummation of our Divine adoption. 'The adoption of sons of God', says St Thomas, 'comes about through a certain conformity of likeness to the image of Him who is His Son by nature.'[6] This is brought about in a two-fold fashion: here below by grace (*per gratiam viae*, grace upon our journey), which is an imperfect conformity; in heaven by glory (*per gloriam patriae*, the glory of our Homeland) – which will be a perfect conformity, according to the saying of St John: 'Dearly beloved, we are now the sons of God; and it hath not yet appeared what we shall be. We know that, when He shall appear, we shall be like to Him: because we shall see Him as He is.'[7]

Here below, then, our divine resemblance is not completed; but in heaven it will appear in its perfection. Here below, we have to labour, in the obscure light of faith, to render ourselves like to God, to 'destroy the old self', to let the 'new self',[8] created in the image of Jesus Christ, unfold: we have to renew ourselves, perfect ourselves, ceaselessly in order to approach the Divine model. In heaven, our divine resemblance will be consummated; we shall see that we are truly children of God.

But this, that we are seeing God, will not put us in the position of an immobile statue, which would prevent our doing anything at all. Contemplation of God will not be the annihilation of our activity. For all that our soul will not cease for a moment to contemplate the Divinity, it will keep free play of all its faculties. Look at Our Lord Jesus Christ. Here on earth, His holy soul constantly enjoyed the Beatific Vision; and yet His human activity was not absorbed by this continual contemplation; it remained intact, it was manifested by His apostolic journeys, preaching and miracles. The perfection of heaven would not be perfection if it had to annihilate the activity of the elect.

We shall see God. Is that all? No: seeing God is the first element of eternal life, the first source of beatitude; but if the intelligence is divinely satisfied by Eternal Truth, must not the will be so, too, by Infinite Goodness? We shall *love* God ... not with a love that is weak, vacillating, so often distracted by creatures, exposed to ruin, but a powerful love, a pure love, a perfect and eternal love. If, in this vale of tears where, to preserve the life of Christ within us, we have to weep and struggle, if here below love is already so strong in certain souls that it rends out of them cries that move us to our depths: 'Who shall separate us from the love of Christ? Neither persecution nor death nor any other creature shall be able to separate us from the love of God'[9] – what will be this love when it embraces, never to lose it, the Infinite Good? What our fervour for God, ceaselessly satisfied! What loving clasping, ceaselessly assuaged! ...

Finally, we shall *joy in* God. You have read in the Gospel that Our Lord Himself compares the kingdom of heaven to a banquet which God has prepared to honour His Son[10] ... What does this signify if not that God will Himself be our joy? 'O Lord,' (cries the Psalmist) the children of men 'shall be inebriated with the plenty of Thy house; and Thou shalt make them drink of the torrent of Thy pleasure. For with Thee is the FOUNTAIN OF LIFE'.[11] God says to the soul that seeks Him: 'It is I – I Myself – who will be your great reward.'[12] It is as if He were saying: 'I have loved you so much that I have not wished to give you a natural bliss, a natural happiness; I have wished to take you into My own house, to adopt you as My child, in order that you might have a share of My own beatitude. I wish you to live by my very life; My own beatitude to become your beatitude. Here below, I have given you My Son, became mortal by His humanity; He was delivered up for you to merit the grace of being and remaining My child; He has given Himself to you in the Eucharist under the veil of faith; now it is I myself in glory who give Myself to you, so as to make you a sharer of My life; to be your beatitude without end.' ...

Our Lord, when He speaks of this beatitude, tells us that God causes the faithful servant to 'enter into the joy of his Lord'.[13] This joy is the joy of God Himself, the joy that God possesses in the knowledge of His infinite perfections, the beatitude that God feels in the ineffable society of the Three Persons; the infinite repose and contentment in which God dwells. His joy will be our joy and 'reach its full measure[14] in us; His beatitude and repose, our beatitude and repose; His life, our life; a perfect life, in which all our faculties will be fully contented.

It is there that will be found 'that full participation in unchangeable good', as St Augustine excellently puts it. To such an extent has God loved us. Oh! if we knew what God has in store for those who love Him!

And because this beatitude and this life are those of God Himself, they will be, for us, eternal. They will have no end, no termination ...

As you know, this life of blessedness becomes the portion of every soul as soon as it goes forth from this world, if it is, by grace, a child of God, and if there does not remain for it anything of the penalty of sin to expiate in Purgatory.

(*Christ, the Life of the Soul*, Part II, XIII, i–ii)

---

[1] 1 Cor. 13:13

[2] 1 Cor. 13:12

[3] Since God the Father and God the Holy Spirit are pure spirit, with what new form of perception does one 'see' them in heaven? How does one 'see' God-the-Son-made-Man, gloriously risen, when one is in that transitional state after death but before the general resurrection when one's body is to be joined to one's soul again? (Or indeed, after the general resurrection?) We do not, I think, know the answers to these questions. – Translator.

[4] 1 John 1:3

[5] See Apoc. 5:9–10, 13

6   See Rom. 8:29: conformed 'to the image of his Son'

7   1 John 3:2

8   See Col. 3:9–10; Eph. 4:22, 24 (old and new 'self', Jerusalem and Knox).

9   See Rom. 8:35

10 Luke 12:37

11 Psalm 35:9 (Jerusalem, 36:8)

12 See Gen. 15:1

13 See Matt. 25:21

14 John 17:13 (Knox)

Marmion as abbot.

Prayers of Blessed Elizabeth and Blessed Columba

BLESSED ELIZABETH'S PRAYER TO THE TRINITY

O my God, Trinity whom I adore, help me to forget myself entirely so as to establish myself in You, as still and peaceful as if my soul were already in eternity. May nothing be able to disturb my peace or make me go out from You, O my Unchanging God! but may each minute take me further into the depths of Your Mystery. Give peace to my soul, make it Your heaven, Your beloved dwelling and the place of Your repose. May I never leave You there alone, but be wholly present, wholly awake in my faith, wholly adoring, wholly yielded up to Your creative Action.

O my beloved Christ, crucified by love, I would like to be a spouse of Your Heart, I would like to cover You with glory, I would like to love You – even to dying of it! But I feel my helplessness, and I ask You to 'clothe me with Yourself', to identify my soul with all the movements of Your soul, to submerge me, to invade me, to substitute Yourself for me, so that my life may be but a radiance of Your Life. Come within me as Adorer, as Restorer and as Saviour. O Eternal Word, Utterance of my God, I wish to spend my life in listening to You, I wish to make myself wholly teachable, so as to learn everything from You. Then, throughout all darkness, all emptiness, all helplessness, I wish to fix my gaze on You always and to live beneath Your great light. O my beloved Star! fascinate me, that I may no longer be able to go out from Your radiance.

O consuming Fire, Spirit of Love, 'come down upon me', that there be brought about in my soul a kind of incarnation of the Word: may I be for Him an added humanity in which He renews all His Mystery. And You, O Father, bend over Your poor little creature, 'cover her with Your shade', see in her only the 'Beloved Son in whom You are well pleased'.

O my Three, my All, my Beatitude, infinite Solitude, Immensity in which I lose myself, I deliver myself up to You as a prey. Bury Yourself in me, that I may bury myself in You, while waiting to go and contemplate in Your Light the abyss of Your greatness.

BLESSED COLUMBA'S PRAYER OF CONSECRATION TO THE TRINITY

O Eternal Father, prostrate in humble adoration at Your feet, we consecrate our whole being to the glory of Your Son Jesus, the Incarnate Word. You have constituted him King of our souls, submit to Him our souls, our hearts, our bodies, and may nothing within us move without His orders, without His inspiration. United with Him, may we be carried into Your bosom, and be consumed in the unity of Your love.

O Jesus, unite us to Yourself in Your life that is altogether holy, altogether consecrated to Your Father and to souls. Be our 'Wisdom, our Justice, our sanctification, our redemption', our *all*. 'Sanctify us in truth'.

O Holy Spirit, love of the Father and the Son, establish Yourself like a furnace of love in the centre of our hearts and ever carry, like blazing flames, our thoughts, our affections, our actions *on high*, within the bosom of the Father. May our whole life be a 'Gloria Patri et Filio et Spiritui Sancto'.

O Mary, Mother of Christ, Mother of Holy Love, yourself form us according to the Heart of your Son.

NOTES TO TRANSLATOR'S INTRODUCTION

Abbreviations

CCC   *Catechism of the Catholic Church*, Geoffrey Chapman, London, 1994. The numerical references are to paragraphs of the Catechism.

HF   *Heaven in Faith*, a spiritual treatise written by Elizabeth in the first half of August 1906. It appeared, abridged, in some editions of the *Souvenirs*. Elizabeth left it untitled; in the *Souvenirs* in English translation it was called 'A Second Retreat'. The full manuscript version in English can be found in Volume One (entitled 'Major Spiritual Writings') of Elizabeth's Complete Works, ICS Publications, Washington DC, 1984.

L   Elizabeth's letters, as numbered in the *Œuvres Complètes* (Les Editions du Cerf, Paris, 1991) and in Volume Two ('Letters from Carmel') of the English translation of the Complete Works (ICS Publications, 1995).

LR   *Last Retreat*, a spiritual treatise written by Elizabeth in the second half of August 1906 and published, a little revised, in the *Souvenirs*. An English translation of the full manuscript version is in ICS's Volume One.

S   The *Souvenirs*, reminiscences of Elizabeth first published at Dijon in 1909 and containing some of her own writings. An English translation, by the Benedictines of Stanbrook, under the title *The Praise of Glory*, was first published in 1913. There was a later English edition, London, Burns & Oates, 1962.

SD   M. M. Philipon, OP, *The Spiritual Doctrine of Elizabeth of the Trinity*, tr. A Benedictine of Stanbrook Abbey (Teresian Charism Press, Washington DC, 1947).

1   Hell does exist (CCC, paras. 1030–1037), though many try to think otherwise or speculate gratuitously that there may be no-one in it. Being in a state of mortal sin (CCC, paras. 1854–1861), however long-lasting, need not be final, since repentance will encounter God's loving mercy until one's very last breath is drawn (1013–1014). But which of us knows when that last breath will come?

2   Karol Wojtyla, *Sign of Contradiction*, XII & XIV (St Paul's Publications, 1979); my italics.

3   S, Ch.IV.

4   Letter to her mother, around 27 May 1906 (L273).

5   Thérèse, at 4, her mother; Elizabeth, at 7, her father. He was an army officer, and Elizabeth was born in an army camp near Bourges.

6   Benedict Zimmerman, ODC, Introduction to the first English translation of the *Souvenirs*.

7   *See*, for example, LR, Third Day: 'If I compare these two accounts of the divine and eternally unchanging plan, I conclude from them that . . .'

8   S, Ch.VIII.

9   But, as Fr. Gregory Collins, OSB, has put it: 'she had an astonishingly refined theological sensibility, and had received very precise conferences in the convent. She has always seemed to me to have had what Marmion called "supernatural tact" and an infused gift of theology derived from prayer.'

10 F. J. Sheed, *Theology and Sanity* (Sheed & Ward, London, 1947), author's foreword.

11 1 John 4:19 (Jerusalem).

12 *Way of Perfection*, Ch.XXVIII, 12 (tr. The Benedictines of Stanbrook).

13 *Spiritual Canticle*, Stanza XIII, 17 (tr. David Lewis).

14 Ch.I.

15 S, Ch.II.

16 *See* Luke 22:42.

17 Poem written in August 1906; p. 126 in this book.

18 Psalm 115(116):15.

19 Stanza I.28 (Lewis); my italics.

20 Thérèse's words; Autobiography, Knox, Ch.XII; Clarke, Ch.IV. Thérèse wanted to fight, spiritually, like Joan of Arc.

21 LR, Second Day.

22 For example: L172, L220 (disappear); L249, quoting St Thérèse, L264, L278, *The Greatness of our Vocation*, 4 (from L310) (forget); L249, L335 (go out from); LR, Eighth Day (despise); L121, LR, Eighth and Thirteenth Days (leave, lose sight of).

23 Gal. 2:20.

24 Above-mentioned poem of August 1906; Psalm 17:20 (Jerusalem 18:19). See also LR, Sixth and Eleventh Days.

25 *Ascent of Mount Carmel*, Book II, vii.8.

26 Letter to Germaine de Gemeaux, 20 September 1903 (L179). An almost identical idea is expressed in the preface to *Meditations on Divine Love* by the seventeenth-century Jesuit, Vincent Huby: '. . . the soul annihilates, as it were, all her desires, subjecting them unreservedly to the absolute disposal of God'. And: 'By love we are taught to forget ourselves that we may remember our sovereign Lord . . . and desire the sole glory of God . . .'

27 L236; L184; L238; L261.

28 John 15:4; see also 1 John 4:16.

29 First Day.

30 Letter to Germaine de Gemeaux, around 10 June 1906 (L278). Elizabeth wrote down and gave to someone (L217) a quotation from Mgr Gay: 'The soul that loves dwells in God, and God dwells in it. Thus, thanks to love and through love, the creature becomes the resting-place of God, and God the resting-place of the creature.'

31 CCC 1260, 1281. 'Baptism of desire' is a concept wider than that of desire for baptism.

32 Encyclical, *Divinum illud munus*, 9 May 1897.

33 1 John 4:8, 16 (Jerusalem).

34 Nicene Creed.

35 The Threeness-in-One defeats our human grammar.

Saying 'He' of God (as we normally do) is less inapt than saying 'They' would be. *See* Translator's Note p. 55.

36 Romance II: Of the communion of the three Persons, tr. Roy Campbell (The Penguin Classics, Penguin Books Ltd., 1960).

37 1 Cor. 13:12.

38 *See* Rom. 8:15, 23; Gal. 4:5; Eph. 1:5.

39 The soul is 'not so much a spirit, wafting upwards from the dead body towards heaven, but the essence of personality: the thing that animates the body, and gives each of us identity and meaning — abilities, traits, foibles, a sense of humour.' (*Daily Telegraph* Leader, Good Friday 2000).

40 1 Cor. 13:12. '*Even as I am known*': 'He has been upstairs and downstairs in the soul and knows every nook and dusty corner', wrote Martin D'Arcy, SJ; He 'is the only one who is in every moment of our lives co-conscious with us.'

41 Referring to the 'profound unions' and 'divine embraces' she experienced even now, what (she exclaimed) would the first face-to-face meeting with Divine Beauty in heaven be like! (Letter to Marthe Weishardt, October 1906: L332).

42 A mystery 'is not something that we can know nothing about: it is only something that the mind cannot *wholly* know' (Sheed, *op. cit.*, Ch.II.ii).

43 L190; L249; L288. See also Marmion's words on pp. 89–90 of this book: 'The Holy Trinity, truly living in us as in a temple, does not remain inactive there . . .'

44 L160. People, remarked Elizabeth, do not know how to wait, if God 'does not give Himself in a perceptible way': L302.

44a 'Come, Lord Jesus!' can mean, for example, 'Come and take possession of my heart and will', rather than 'Come where you were not before'.

45 His spiritual letters, Letter V (1734).

46 *Relations*, III.6 (tr. Lewis). See also, as to her infused *perception* of the indwelling, *Relations*, III.9 and 13; *Interior Castle*, VII Mansions, Ch.1, 9ff.

47 S, Ch.XIV. The Mother Prioress, Mère Germaine, was the

author of the *Souvenirs*, so the account of what Elizabeth said to her is first-hand. One wonders whether there is not some associative significance in the fact that both St Teresa's experience and Elizabeth's took place around the time of the Feast of the Ascension. Jesus, after the Last Supper, said: 'I go to the Father ... And I will ask the Father, and He shall give you another Paraclete' (John 14:13, 16), referring to the coming of the Holy Spirit to the Church.

48 SD, Ch.III. 2. 'In the beginning', Philipon says (Ch.VIII.1), the Christian 'moves "in the family of God" rather like an adopted child who has not yet become used to its new home.'

49 L196; and L198. In L112 Elizabeth spoke of a First Communion as a union 'begun between Jesus and His little communicant'.

50 John, 15:1–8.

51 Hans Urs von Balthasar, *Two Sisters in the Spirit* (Ignatius Press, San Francisco, 1992), Second Part on Elizabeth, tr. Dennis D. Martin, Introduction.

52 *See* note 32.

53 My italics.

54 'Appropriation', a theological term, is here referred to. Sheed: 'The operations of the Divine Nature upon the created universe and everything within it are the operations of the Three Divine Persons acting as one principle, not of any one or other of them ... There is *no* external operation of the Divine Nature which is the work of one Person as distinct from the others. Yet both the New Testament and the Church's Liturgy are packed with phrases which do seem to attribute certain divine operations to Father or Son or Holy Ghost ... We are encouraged to attribute this or that external operation of the Blessed Trinity to that Person to whom the corresponding operation *within the Godhead* belongs ... If we always thought of the operation of God upon us as the operation of all three Persons, we should be in danger of regarding

the three Persons as only a form of words, with no distinction of one from another ... Whereas appropriation to one Person or another continually reminds us of the distinction: and the specific appropriations that we make remind us that the Father is Origin and Power, the Son Knowledge or Wisdom, the Holy Ghost Love. Thus each Person is for us a distinct reality, and the reality that He really is. Provided we keep clear in our minds the complementary truth that the action appropriated to each Person is in fact the action of all Three, then there is only gain for us.' (Sheed, *op. cit.*, Ch.IX.ii; italics in twelfth and thirteenth lines mine).

55 *See also* 1 Cor. 3:16: 'Know you not that you are the temple of God, and that the Spirit of God dwelleth in you?'

56 Letter to Germaine de Gemeaux, 20 August 1903 (L172). In a poem of May 1902 (P79) she writes, of the Annunciation, that the Spirit of Love covers Mary with His shade, 'the Three come to her'.

57 For example, HF, Fourth Day: 'the Hearth-Fire of love which burns in us, and is none other than the Holy Spirit, that same Love which in the Trinity is the bond of the Father and His Word.'

58 This phrase refers to her spiritual treatises. For example, in *Heaven in Faith*, First Day, Elizabeth alludes to St John of the Cross's reference to Hosea (Osee) 2:14 when she writes: 'the solitude into which God wants to allure the soul that He may speak to it' (*see Spiritual Canticle*, Note to St. XXXIV; also *Living Flame of Love*, St. III.38, Lewis). In the *Œuvres Complètes* the term 'Private Notes' is reserved for the private notes other than those, including *Heaven in Faith* and the *Last Retreat*, which have been classified as 'Major Spiritual Writings'.

59 SD, Ch.III.2.

60 *The Ascent of Mount Carmel*, Book II, Ch.V.3 (Lewis), my italics. See also Marmion, *Christ, the Life of the Soul*, Part I, VI.iv.

61 Père Marie-Eugène, OCD, *I Want to See God*, tr. Sister M.

Verda Clare, CSC (Christian Classics, Inc., Westminster Md., 1953, Ch.II, 2 and 3).

62 Ch.XXVIII.10 (tr. The Benedictines of Stanbrook).

63 For example, St Teresa of Avila, *op. cit.*, Ch.XXVIII, 11. Cf. 'I have run the way of thy commandments, when thou didst enlarge my heart': Psalm 118 (119):32.

64 That is, in addition to the metaphor of dilation of the heart, which she uses also: L180; L219, after her entry to Carmel; and in a number of poems before that time.

65 Letter to the Abbé Chevignard, 29 November 1904 (L214).

66 Letter to her mother, August 29, 1906 (L308).

67 Letter to Louise Demoulin, around end of June 1906 (L291).

68 SD, Ch.VIII.1.

69 *The Doctrine of the Divine Indwelling; a Commentary on the Prayer of Sister Elizabeth of the Trinity* (The Mercier Press, Cork, 1950), pp. 17–18.

70 Book II, Ch.V.4 (Lewis).

71 *The Living Flame of Love*, Stanza III.25 (Lewis).

72 'He that eateth my flesh, and drinketh my blood, hath everlasting life' (John 6:55). 'The mode of Christ's presence under the Eucharistic species is unique ... it is presence in the fullest sense' (CCC1474). Sanctifying grace ('a state of grace') is a condition precedent for worthy reception of the Eucharist.

73 *Op. cit.*, Letter V.

74 G. K. Chesterton, essay entitled 'If I had only One Sermon to Preach' ('it would be a sermon against Pride').

75 Robert M. Garrity, *O Happy Fault* (Paulist Press, New York, 1994).

76 LR, Seventh Day.

77 S, Ch.XIV; LR, Fifteenth Day.

78 Eph.1:12. (Knox: 'we were to manifest his glory').

79 'I have found my vocation there', declared Elizabeth after reading St Paul; 'since I shall be the praise of glory eternally, I want to be *laudem gloriae* starting here below' (S, Ch.VIII); L256; LR, First Day.

80 S, Ch.XVII.

81 Col. 3:3.

82 I like the wording of a prayer of St Thomas More's, which asks for 'a love of Thee *incomparably above the love of myself*'. On the one hand this delicate and lovely wording does not exclude self-interest on the part of the person praying (our interests and God's desires for us being the same). On the other hand, and primarily, it emphasizes where fulfilment of self is to be found, i.e. in God and not in oneself. Later in the same prayer he says: 'Give me, Lord, a longing to be with Thee, not for . . . the attaining (of) the joys of Heaven [which is self-related] as purely for the love of Thee.'

83 SD, Ch.IV, opening section.

84 LR, Eighth Day.

85 1 John 3:2 (Jerusalem).

86 1 Cor. 2:9; Isaiah 64:4.

87 'Glory', writes the Scripture scholar Fr Stephen Redmond, SJ, 'is one of the great words of the Bible and of Christian tradition. The Hebrew word is *kabod* . . . A person's *kabod* is his or her importance or dignity – that which demands the respect of others. Applied to God, *kabod* and its Greek equivalent *doxa* mean God himself in so far as he reveals himself.' (*The Music of the Gospel*, Kings Abbot Press, Preston, 1999). Thus, simply *how things are* – gloriously are – as regards God. Not any arrogation of importance or dignity as it would be with us.

88 Sheed, *op. cit.*, Ch.I.1.

89 The present book does not have the purpose of proving the existence of God, our creaturehood and the existence and immortality of the soul. The arguments are set out in other books. Quite apart from what is written in the heart, I say that there is overwhelming evidence for the existence of God (e.g. my physical eye and yours as a precision instrument of sight; ridiculous to think that this came into being by chance!), as well as firm historical evidence for the resurrection of Jesus Christ.

90   *A Catechism of Catholic Doctrine*, Jubilee Edition (Catholic Truth Society, London, 1999), para. 136.

91   Letter to Françoise de Sourdon, around 12 August 1905 (L238).

92   St Bernard of Clairvaux, *On the Song of Songs*, 83.1. Garrity quotes this splendid passage.

93   *See* SD, Ch.IV.3.

94   'God not only created man for His greater glory, but likewise for the purpose of contracting with him a tender and indissoluble union.' (Huby).

95   John 15:5.

95a One's actions and progress depend, not partly upon oneself and partly upon God, but wholly upon oneself and wholly upon God.

96   HF, First Day; LR, First Day.

97   CCC 846–848.

98   John 10:30.

99   SD, Ch.V.5.

100 L109; L123; L330; L333. 'Heaven in faith', another phrase of hers, is distinguished from the face-to-face in eternity.

101 HF, Tenth Day. Her quotation is from St John of the Cross, *Spiritual Canticle*, St. XII.8.

102 1 Cor. 2:10.

103 LR, Eighth Day; see also Third Day.

104 John 15:4.

105 HF, First Day. It was written of St Aloysius Gonzaga that he lived in 'so close a union with His Divine Majesty that he never said or did anything without the consciousness of the Divine Presence'.

106 Letter to Louise Demoulin, around end of June 1906 (L291).

107 Letter to Madame Angles, 15 February 1903 (L16); Elizabeth's emphasis.

108 See *Spiritual Canticle*, St.XII.8 (Lewis).

109 HF, Third Day. The Liturgy, addressing God the Father, has the phrase: 'that You may see and love in us what You

see and love in Christ'. In the poem of St John of the Cross quoted from on p. 13 above, resemblance to the Son is the measure of what 'satisfies Me truly', the poet makes the Father say.

110   *Spiritual Canticle*, St.XII.7 (Lewis).

111   Treatise *On union with God*, attributed to Blessed Albert the Great, Ch.12; L194. To 'go out from ourselves' is a phrase used by Ruysbroeck.

112   Letter to Madame Angles, around 26 November 1905 (L249).

113   L287; L161. St Teresa of Avila wrote: 'Wherever God dwells, there is heaven . . . We are not forced to take wings to find Him, but have only to seek solitude and to look within ourselves.' (*The Way of Perfection*, Ch. XXVIII.1–2).

114   Letter to Sœur Marie-Odile, 28 October 1906 (L335).

115   'Then one is never alone any more . . .' (L161).

116   Letter to the Abbé Chevignard, 27 April 1904 (L199); and Prayer to the Trinity.

117   L249.

118   Letter to the Abbé Chevignard, 25 January 1904 (L191).

119   L335 (adhere); L293 (gaze); LR, Sixth Day (live habitually); L252 (be rooted, quoting St Paul); L121 (surrender).

120   Letter to Madame de Sourdon, 25 July 1902 (L129).

121   L145; L165.

122   Letter to Mathilde Rolland, October 1902 (L139). *See also* LR, Eighth Day.

123   Letter to Canon Angles, around 27 August 1903 (L177).

124   From a longer version of P 85.

125   Letter to Germaine de Gemeaux, 20 August 1903 (L172).

126   HF, Fifth Day.

127   Marmion, Conference, Maredret, 1916; quoted in Philipon, *The Spiritual Doctrine of Dom Marmion*, tr. Dom Matthew Dillion, OSB (Sands & Co. (Publishers) Ltd., London, 1956), Part II.

128   *Christ, the Life of the Soul*, Part II, VIII.ii. In translating, I have taken the meaning here to be transformation 'in', not

'into', Christ; in this passage Marmion wrote 'transformation dans', not 'en' as elsewhere.

129   For example, L1341: 'the divine fusion', of the soul and God. See also L169; L175.

130   St Bernard: see note 142. St John of the Cross, *The Living Flame of Love*, St.II.40 (Lewis); my italics.

131   L231; L 274.

132   '*Lovers' exaggeration*': Seeking to avoid misunderstanding, I am uneasy when I read Elizabeth (and Marmion too) saying 'transformation *into* Christ. My lawyerly pen wants always to add some qualifying clause to this. Ruysbroeck insisted: 'We cannot wholly become God and lose our created being, it is impossible'. When he wrote of our becoming 'one with God', he meant, he said, 'one in love, not in essence and nature'.

Marmion himself wrote: 'Our nature supposes that the *creature* remain always in most humble adoration before the Creator: that is so essential that *nothing* can change it. Our adoption to the state of child of God raises our nature, but does not destroy it.' (*Union with God*, I.; Marmion's italics). In HF, Second Day, Elizabeth refers to words of St John of the Cross: in the divine union on earth 'all the movements of such a soul are divine, and though of God, *still they are the soul's* . . .'; the soul wills and assents (*The Living Flame of Love*, Stanza I, 10–11, Lewis; my italics)

Blessed Albert the Great wrote: 'Love, *if it could*, would form but one being with the Beloved.' . . . Lover and loved, 'each passes into the other, *as far as is possible*.' In the same chapter he has written, with caution, of transformation '*into His likeness*' (*On Union with God*, Ch. 12: my italics).

When Elizabeth, in a letter to Canon Angles (L294) asked the latter 'to consecrate me at Holy Mass as a sacrifice (*hostie*) of praise to the glory of God . . . so that I may be *no longer I, but Him*', she was, of course, using the language of devotional hyperbole. Had she really been asserting the possibility of a change of our human substance into God, directly comparable to the change of the substance of the bread and wine at Mass, that would not have been a defensible proposition.

133 John 14:15 (Jerusalem). Elizabeth wrote: 'Love – that is what attracts, what draws God down to His creatures: not a love of the feelings, but that love 'strong as death, and that many waters cannot quench,': HF, Third Day. The joy of her soul was 'as to the will, not for the feelings': *ibid.*

134 Matt. 7:21.

135 John 15:11 (Jerusalem).

136 *'If any one love Me* . . . my Father and I will love him, and we will come to him' (John 14:23). 'Behold, I stand at the gate, and knock' (Apoc. 3:20).

137 Diary, 11 March; 25 March 1899.

138 HF, Third Day.

139 *See* John 8:29.

140 Letter to Clémence Blanc, July 1906 (L293).

141 Letter to her sister, 24 June 1906 (L288).

142 St Bernard, *On the Song of Songs*, Serm. LXXXIII.3; *Treatise on the Love of God*, 28, both quoted and expounded on by Dom Godefroid Bélorgey, OCSO in *The Practice of Mental Prayer* (The Mercier Press, Cork, 1951), XV.5.

143 Note by Marmion, 1900; given in *Abbot Columba Marmion: a Master of the Spiritual Life* by Dom Raymund Thibaut, OSB, translated by Mother Mary St Thomas (Sands & Co., London, 1932).

144 'like to' (the Douai's phrase), 1 John 3:2.

145 Poem written in 1902 (p. 92 of this book).

146 Letter of 11 June 1902 to Sœur Agnès de Jésus-Maria (L121). Marmion wrote: 'sanctifying grace . . . so to speak, deifies our nature and renders it capable of acting supernaturally'. (*Christ, the Life of the Soul*, Part I, VI.iv).

147 *See* John 12:24–25.

148 'What the good God asks of you is never to stay *voluntarily* with any prideful thought . . . And yet, if you notice (this in yourself) there is no need to be discouraged, for it's pride again that is being irritated . . .' (*The Greatness of Our Vocation*, 5; Elizabeth's emphasis).

149   Diary, 24 March 1899.
150   L264; L298; HF, Fourth Day; 1 Cor. 15:31.
151   Bélorgey, *op. cit.*, XV.5, referring to St Bernard, *Treatise on the Love of God*, 28.
152   Poem written in July 1906 (p. 82 of this book). In a letter, she wrote that when we love 'we no longer belong to ourselves' (L229) but to the loved one.
153   Col. 3:3.
154   Recall that the word 'mortification' comes from the root *mors*, death (of self). 'If (the grain of wheat) die, it bringeth forth much fruit . . . he that hateth his life in this world, keepeth it unto life eternal' (John 12:25). St Francis of Assisi: 'Teach me to hate myself, that I may love Thee.'
155   LR, Sixth Day.
156   Letter to Germaine de Gemeaux, 20 September 1903 (L179).
157   Letter to her mother, 2 August 1902 (L130).
158   Poem written for Christmas 1903 (p. 64 of this book).
159   Poem written in 1902 (p. 98 of this book).
160   Poem written for September 29 1906 (p. 105 of this book).
161   Poem written for Christmas 1904 (p. 117 of this book).
162   Diary, 27 January 1900. This, as Father Conrad de Meester has pointed out, echoes 'Thérèse had disappeared . . . Jesus only remained' (St Thérèse's autobiography).
163   Poem written in August 1906 (p. 127 of this book).
164   Gal. 2:20 (Knox).
165   Letter to Madame Angles, 15 February 1903 (L156).
166   Letter to Madame Angles, February or March 1905 (L224).
167   Letter to Marguerite Gollot, July 19 1901 (L73).
168   Suffering was something which Elizabeth neither enjoyed in itself nor was anaesthetized to: '. . . not to be occupied with oneself . . . doesn't consist in no longer feeling one's physical or mental woes': L249.
169   *Introduction à la spiritualité de Sainte Thérèse de l'Enfant Jésus,*

200

as cited in translation in Père François Jamart, OCD, *Complete Spiritual Doctrine of St Thérèse of Lisieux*, tr. Walter van de Putte, CSSP. (Alba House, New York, 1961).

170 Letter to her mother, 11 July, 1906 (L295).
171 Letter to her mother, 29 August, 1906 (L308).
172 Poem written for St Martha's Day, 1905 (p. 135 of this book).
173 Letter to Germaine de Gemeaux, 7 August 1902 (L133); Elizabeth's emphasis.
174 *See* p. 154 of this book.
175 Fr Francis Marsden, article in *The Catholic Times*. Elizabeth wrote to her mother: 'you're afraid ... that I might be a victim marked out for suffering. I beg you not to be sad about it, that would be so beautiful; I don't feel worthy of it' (L300).
176 Letter to her Rolland aunts, January 1906 (L258).
177 Diary, 31 March 1899.
178 Diary, 9 March 1899. She added: 'O Jesus, my Spouse and my Life, give me crosses, I want to share them with You, ah, do not suffer without me.'
179 Diary, 7 March 1899.
180 Diary, 30 January 1899.
181 Letter to Françoise de Sourdon, October–November 1901 (L98).
182 19 June 1902 (L123).
183 *See Poems of St Thérèse of Lisieux*, tr. Alan Bancroft (HarperCollins, 1996), pp. xxxvi and xxxix; *Collected Poems of St Thérèse of Lisieux* (Gracewing, 2001), pp. xxxi and xxxiv.
184 'Gloria Patri' is a shorthand phrase for the prayer of which those are the first words. In Marmion's a *Consecration to the Blessed Trinity* (Christmas, 1908), the phrase is expanded: 'May our whole life be a *Gloria Patri et Filio et Spiritui Sancto*', Glory be to the Father and to the Son and to the Holy Spirit.
185 In L182 there is a reference to a French Carmel (unidentified) which was exiled from France, to the members of which 'our Mothers of Belgium' (not further identified)

had given refuge. The Belgian Mothers had organized a raffle in aid of the exiled Carmel's support, and Elizabeth sends to her friend Françoise some of the raffle tickets, which the Prioress of Dijon has asked her to enclose.

186   This prayer forms the basis of a book of Marmion's writings edited by Dom Raymund Thibaut, OSB, and entitled *Consécration à la Sainte Trinité*. An English translation of that book, entitled *The Trinity in our Spiritual Life*, was published in 1953 (The Mercier Press, Cork).

187   Thibaut, *Abbot Columba Marmion: A Master of the Spiritual Life*, Ch.IV.

188   Ch.IX. The relevant page of the *Souvenirs* simply refers to Elizabeth's being 'fully recollected under the grace of' the quotation. But in two of her letters (L165 and 193) Elizabeth mentions that 'someone' (unidentified) wrote to her giving the quotation.

189   'During a meeting with his clergy, he warmly recommended the book to them and expressed the wish that it might find a place in the library of every one of his priests.' (SD, Introduction; Philipon does not assign a date to this meeting.)

190   Marmion refers to it in a footnote to *Christ, the Life of the Soul*, Part I, VI, opening section.

191   Dom Savinien Louismet, OSB, *The Burning Bush*, Burns Oates & Washbourne, London, 1926. Louismet uses 'ecstatical' in a special sense, not the ordinary one.

192   For details of the latter of these works by Philipon see note 127 above.

193   Thibaut, Preface to Philipon's *The Spiritual Doctrine of Dom Marmion*.

194   Philipon, *ibid.*, Part II.

195   SD, Ch.III. Thibaut's words on Marmion parallel those of Philipon's on Elizabeth most remarkably: Marmion's Trinitarian writings of 1906 were 'written with a single stroke of the pen, rapidly and without corrections' (Thibaut's foreword to *The Trinity in our Spiritual Life*).

The following are fuller details of sources:

Biblical quotations are from the Douai version unless otherwise indicated.

The passage from the Venerable John Henry Newman (p. 60 above) comes from his book *The Arians of the Fourth Century*, Ch.II.iii.

G.K. Chesterton's essay 'If I had only One Sermon to Preach', which contains the passages quoted on pp. 22 and 108–109 above, was published in the collection of his essays, *The Common Man*, London, 1950, by Sheed & Ward, to whom I give an acknowledgement both formal and grateful.

The English Religious Heritage by Conrad Pepler, OP, from which the extracts on pp. 118, 130 and 170 are taken, was published in 1958 by the Aquin Press, London. For the appearance of these extracts here I am very grateful to the Very Rev. Allan White, OP, Prior Provincial of the Dominican English Province.

I am indebted in many places to the critical notes of Father Conrad de Meester, OCD, in the *Œuvres Complètes* of Elizabeth (Les Editions du Cerf, Paris, 1991).

The illustrations appear through the kind co-operation of the Prioress of the Dijon Carmel and of Dom Mark Tierney, OSB, Vice-Postulator, in relation to Blessed Elizabeth and Blessed Columba respectively. The photograph of Elizabeth on the front cover shows her in a postulant's veil three days after her entry into Carmel in August 1901.